COLLECTING
AMERICAN
DINNERWARE

Joe L. Rosson

HOUSE OF COLLECTIBLES

NEW YORK

Instant Expert: Collecting American Dinnerware
by Joe L. Rosson

Copyright © 2004 by Random House Inc.

This book is available for special discounts for bulk purchases for sales promotions or premiums. Special editions, including personalized covers, excerpts of existing books, and corporate imprints, can be created in large quantities for special needs. For more information, write to Special Markets/Premium Sales, 1745 Broadway, MD 6-2, New York, NY, 10019 or e-mail specialmarkets@randomhouse.com.

Please address inquiries about electronic licensing of reference products for use on a network, in software or on CD-ROM to the Subsidiary Rights Department, Random House Reference, fax 212-572-6003.

Visit the Random House Web site: www.randomhouse.com

Library of Congress Cataloging-in-Publication Data is available.

First Edition

0 9 8 7 6 5 4 3 2 1

ISBN: 0-375-72057-X

CONTENTS

ACKNOWLEDGMENTS

No book is written by just one person. There are always people who contribute their advice, their support, and their skills. For this particular book, Rick Crane was indispensable for his input, his editing skills, and his photography. Helaine Fendelman, my longtime cohost on *Treasures in Your Attic*, for her careful editing and timely introduction to Random House. Elaine Tomber Tindell (producer of *Treasures in Your Attic*) for her unflagging friendship, her inexhaustible enthusiasm for collecting, and her willingness to allow her collection of dinnerware to be photographed. The talented Annie Parrott for her incredibly detailed line drawings. Chris Paddleford and Kingston Pike Antique Mall in Knoxville, Tennessee, for allowing access to the mall's pieces of American everyday dinnerware for photographic purposes, and Scott Houston for his technical assistance and expertise.

All illustrations by Annie Parrott

All photographs by Richard Crane

INTRODUCTION

What Is an Instant Expert?

An instant expert in the field of American everyday dinnerware needs to be able to recognize the most desirable patterns, such as Hall's "Autumn Leaf," Homer Laughlin's "Fiesta," Gladding, McBean's "Desert Rose," Taylor, Smith and Taylor's "Lu-Ray Pastels," Metlox's "Red Rooster," Vernon Kilns' "Salamina," and Southern Potteries' "French Peasant." An instant expert also needs to know the most sought-after and rarest shapes, and how an uncommon color and scarce form can sometimes interplay to create a very valuable collectible.

The term "American everyday dinnerware" refers to the earthenware table settings that were made primarily during the mid-20th century (1925–1975) and designed to be used on a daily basis at breakfast, lunch, and dinner by the typical American family. These were the dishes that Mom or Grandma pulled out of the kitchen cabinet to serve an after-school PB&J sandwich or to hold countless pieces of Monday night meatloaf and Tuesday night fish sticks.

For the most part, these pieces were not meant to set a formal table for company, but they were—or could be—stylish, colorful, and attractive. This sort of dinnerware is familiar and comfortable and can conjure up images of families having dinner together.

American everyday dinnerware was made in relatively large quantities by a large number of manufacturers, and almost every household had at least one set. Today, these pieces have become far more collectible than much of the more elegant porcelain dinner sets that were produced during the same time period—and in many cases, are far more valuable.

In this book, we will take a very concise look at American everyday dinnerware, its makers, its designs, its colors, and its forms. The first important hint to consider is that the items that make up the standard components of a dinnerware service, such as plates, soup bowls, cups, and saucers, are likely to be relatively common and, therefore, less valuable than accessory pieces, such as lazy Susans, covered casseroles, candlesticks, and coffeepots. The exceptions to this might be when a plate comes in a rare color or when a soup bowl has a type of rim that is not the standard configuration.

1

THINK AND TALK
LIKE AN EXPERT

No one is exactly sure when the first pottery was made in the area that would become known as the United States of America during the waning years of the 18th century. There is no reason to debate that here, but it is important to know that until the late 19th century the ceramics industry in the United States played a very subservient role to European makers.

Until this time, if Americans wanted to can or store food, they bought utilitarian crocks and jugs from the country potter in the area where they lived. However, if they wanted to set their table with either porcelain or earthenware dishes, they wanted them to be European—primarily English, French, or German. After the Civil War, two great pottery centers began to develop in the United

States, one around Trenton, New Jersey, and the other around East Liverpool, Ohio. Later, the area around Los Angeles developed as another region where significant amounts of pottery were manufactured.

In the 19th century, many of the makers in these centers tried to disguise the fact that their wares were made in the United States by marking their products with symbols and names that might confuse buyers into thinking that the pieces were actually made in Europe. The Sevres China Company, for example, used the word "Sevres" and a fleur-de-lis in imitation of the French porcelain maker, and the Pottery Co-Operative of East Liverpool, Ohio, commonly marked their wares with the name "Dresden," after the German city where Europeans discovered how to make Chinese-style hard-paste porcelain in 1709.

The practice of using European-sounding names continued, to some extent, into the 20th century, when such deception was no longer quite as necessary. A good example might be the Limoges China Company, which is located in Sebring, Ohio, and not in Limoges, France, as the name implies. When the word "Limoges" is used, consumers immediately think of the vast quantities of fine-quality porcelain dinnerware that were manufactured for at least two centuries in the famous French city. They do not think of Sebring, Ohio.

The **Limoges China Company** was founded in 1901, when it was still a good idea for American ceramics makers to conjure up images of European products and quality in the minds of their customers. At the time, "Limoges" was a very powerful name with the American consumer, and there were few middle- and upper-income households in the United States that did not have at least one set of the fine porcelain dinnerware made by any one of a number of different companies that were located in or around Limoges, France.

To be fair to the Limoges China Company, they did clearly mark their wares with such designations as "American Limoges" and "Limoges Sebring, Ohio." Still, there was a vast difference in quality be-tween the French and the Amer-ican products, with the French companies making the superior ware by a wide margin.

The American Limoges China Company either had high ambi-tions that they never fulfilled or simply wanted to associate themselves with a name that pushed a positive psychological "hot button" with buyers of din-nerware. In any event, some of today's novice collectors find the American products marked "Limoges" to be a bit confusing.

British royal coat of arms used by the Willets Manufacturing Company of Trenton, New Jersey, on stone china in the late 19th century.

By far, the ersatz mark that was most frequently used to mislead American buyers into buying American prod-ucts was one that was very reminiscent of the British royal coat of arms. The list of companies that employed this deceptive symbol is very long indeed and includes the Steubenville Pottery Company of Steubenville, Ohio; Empire Pottery of Trenton, New Jersey; Vodrey Pottery of East Liverpool, Ohio; the American China Company of Toronto, Ohio; and the Akron China Company of Akron, Ohio, among a number of others.

It was not until near the turn of the 20th century that Americans were widely buying sets of dinnerware for their tables that were made by American companies. The pieces now being most avidly collected by current collec-tors, however, were not introduced until the 1920s and 1930s, and they were intended to be mass-produced and widely distributed to large numbers of consumers.

Talking the Talk

Before American everyday dinnerware can be discussed properly, a vocabulary of important terms and concepts needs to be established. It is important, for instance, to know the difference between pottery and porcelain and what a dealer means when he refers to a "coupe shape" or a "lug soup."

The word "pottery" can be defined as any item made from clay that has been baked in a fire or kiln or even hardened in the sun. Technically, this rather broad term encompasses other words, such as "china," "earthenware," "porcelain," and "stoneware." However, most people who use the word "pottery" tend to exclude china, porcelain, and stoneware from this otherwise very inclusive designation.

Most collectors feel that china, porcelain, and stoneware are their own categories and that "pottery" actually refers to any clay product that is opaque, soft enough that it can be scratched with a steel knife blade, and porous to the point that it will not hold water without being covered with a glaze. Pottery is generally fired at a relatively low temperature and in some instances can be hardened in the sun.

"Hard-paste" porcelain, which is sometimes called "china" in reference to the country where it was first made, refers to objects that are crafted using special types of ingredients. One of these materials is a white clay called kaolin—also known as "china clay"—and the other is petuntse, or "china stone," which is feldspar.

Hard-paste porcelain may be translucent but does not have to be. It will hold water without having a glaze and is so hard that it cannot be scratched by the steel blade of a knife. It is fired at very high temperatures that usually range between 1,300 and 1,450 degrees Celsius.

There is another type of porcelain, called "soft-paste" porcelain, that was first made in Europe during the 18th century. This is actually an artificial porcelain that was made by adding "frit" (i.e., ground glass), soapstone, or bone ash (thus the term "bone china") into white clay. The resulting product is softer than hard-paste porcelain, can be scratched with the steel blade of a knife, and is generally very translucent, showing a faint green, gray, or orange color when a light is shown through it.

As mentioned previously, this book discusses only American dinnerware that is made from pottery—specifically earthenware and hybrids such as ironstone and "semi-porcelain"—and what follows are some words you need to know.

Backstamp
The mark or logo found on the bottom or reverse side of a ceramic item. It can be printed or stamped in ink or

transfer printed either under or over the glaze. In addition, it can be impressed into the body of the clay. Backstamps can be very important identification tools, but they should not be relied on entirely when deciding the age and authenticity of a piece of pottery or porcelain.

Backstamp

Baker
An oval dish used for baking food in the oven and also for serving at the table. These generally do not have covers.

Batter Set
A set consisting of a jug for holding waffle batter, a syrup pitcher, and a tray. These originated when electric waffle makers were introduced into the American home as "must-have" modern conveniences. Soon, it became fashionable to make waffles at the dining table rather than at the stove. Making them in the dining room or even at the breakfast table in the kitchen required attractive equipment to go along with the shiny new waffle maker, and the batter set was born.

Bisque
The first firing given to a piece of pottery is called the "bisque firing," and a piece that is only fired once and has no glaze on it is called "bisque ware."

Blank
A piece of pottery (porcelain or earthenware) that has not yet been decorated but is intended to be. Blanks were often sold by manufacturers to amateur china painters, who would then apply a decoration of their own design.

Bouillon Cup
A two-handled cup resembling a teacup that is used to serve clear soups. It is typically accompanied by a saucer.

Casserole
A round or oval baking dish with a cover that is also used at the table as a serving dish.

Baker

Casting

Method of forming ceramic objects in which liquid clay, called "slip," is poured into a mold made from plaster of Paris. The water in the slip is absorbed into the plaster of Paris leaving a thin layer of clay on the inside walls of the mold. How much clay that is deposited depends on the amount of time the slip is left in the mold. After a period of time, the remaining slip is poured out and a clay shape that conforms to the mold is left. The mold is then taken apart and the clay object removed.

Chop Plate

A round serving platter resembling a dinner plate only larger, with a 12- to 16-inch diameter.

Compote

A bowl with a stem or shaft that is designed to hold candy, fruit, or other sweets.

Console Set

A three-piece set intended to be used in the center of a dining room table. It consists of a bowl for flowers and two candlesticks that were to be placed on either side of the bowl.

Coupe

A modern shape that does not have a pronounced rim or shoulder. Pieces with a coupe shape are essentially flat, but they roll up slightly at the edge. This term is generally used to describe soup bowls, plates, and platters.

Bouillon Cup

Casserole

Cozy Set
A set of two rectangular pitchers on a tray. One pitcher has a short spout and is for hot water, while the other has a longer spout and is designed to hold tea.

Crackle
A network of tiny cracks that was induced at the time of manufacture as a decorative effect and is not a defect.

Compote

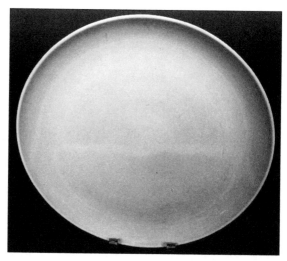

Coupe

Crazing

A network of tiny cracks that is generally caused during the manufacturing process when the glaze and the body do not "fit" and one contracts more than the other, causing the glaze to develop this characteristic system of tiny cracks. Also, this can happen over time and use and is caused by excessive heat or moisture getting underneath the glaze. Crazing is considered to be a defect in many

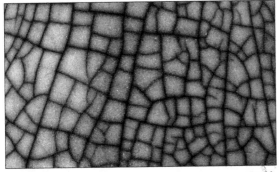

Crackle

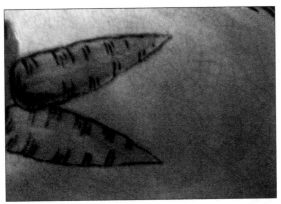

Crazing

cases, and collectors will sometimes reject a piece that is crazed.

Cream Soup

A two-handled cup used to hold thick, cream-based soup. It has an accompanying saucer and is broader and flatter than a bouillon cup.

Decal

A design, either multicolored or monochromatic, that is printed on a special type of paper that may or may not be coated with plastic. Then the area to be decorated is covered with size (a kind of gelatinous substance made from glue, wax, or clay) and the paper decal is positioned on the ceramic item to be decorated. The design adheres

Decal

Embossing

to the size, and when the piece is fired in the kiln, this decoration becomes permanently incorporated into the glaze. The decal is a modern version of transfer printing.

Embossing
A raised decoration achieved by the molding process and not applied separately to the body.

Finial

Engobe

A decorative technique in which slip (liquid clay) is put on the body of a piece before the final glaze is applied. The slip may be white or colored.

Finial

In ceramics, the knob on top of a lid that is grasped in order to remove it. In the larger sense, a finial is any decorative knob on top of something, such as a lampshade, an arch, or a bedpost.

Firing

The process of heating ceramic objects in a kiln to harden them, give them strength, affix decoration or gilding, and/or make the shape permanent. An item might go through several firings for different purposes and at different temperatures before it is finished.

Flatware

Items that are primarily flat, such as plates and platters. In silver, this term refers to the place setting of knives, forks, and spoons.

French Casserole

A casserole with a single, long sticklike handle. This type of casserole dish comes in a variety of sizes, and the larger ones often have a lug handle opposite the stick handle to aid in picking up, handling, and stabilizing the vessel.

French Casserole

Gadroon

Gadroon
A band of raised ornamentation usually placed around or near the rim of a plate, bowl, or other vessel that often consists of elements resembling ovals and straight lines.

Gilding
The process of applying gold or platinum (for the look of silver) to ceramics for decorative purposes.

Glaze
A mixture of minerals and water that is applied to the surface of a piece of ceramic in order to seal a porous

Grill Plate

body and make it impervious to liquids or to achieve a decorative effect. Glazes also help protect the surface, and they can be clear or colored.

Gloss Glaze
A shiny glaze that has a reflective, mirrorlike surface.

Green Ware
Ceramic wares that have been formed either on a wheel or in a mold and are not yet fired. In the green ware state, the pieces are allowed to dry, and the ceramic body, which is fragile and easily damaged, is said to be "leather hard." After the pieces are fired for the first time, green ware becomes bisque ware.

Grill Plate
A plate divided with ridges into three or more sections. These are usually the same size as a dinner plate—about 8 to 10 inches in diameter.

Hollowware
As opposed to flatware, ceramic pieces that have raised sides and are hollow inside. Hollowware includes such things as pitchers, bowls, casseroles, and cups.

Ironstone

A hard, nonporous ceramic body that was made using ground stone. It is stronger than regular earthenware bodies and has been given a variety of names over the years, many of which were chosen to imply to the user that the pieces were strong and durable. The most widely used was "white granite" or "graniteware."

Jigger

A device used to form plates and other flatware objects. This is a modification of a potter's wheel in which a disk of clay is revolved on a turning platform and then shaped with an arm or a shaped blade that removes part of the clay leaving the desired shape of a plate or platter.

Kiln

An ovenlike device for firing ceramics, glazes, and decorations. One type of kiln is a "tunnel kiln," which is a long heated tunnel down which pieces of pottery travel for a predetermined length of time at a preset temperature. This is a fairly modern industrial type of kiln that was reportedly developed during the 1920s. Another type of kiln is called a "muffle kiln," which has a chamber lined with firebrick. The pottery is placed in this chamber, and the heat source or fire is on the other side of the bricks so the flames and ash will be kept away from the wares being fired. A "glost kiln" is one used for firing glazes.

Lug Handle

A long, flat, tablike handle found on bowls. They normally are placed on the bowl parallel to the tabletop, and they may be solid or pierced. When these are found on a bowl resembling a cream soup bowl, the piece is often called a "lug soup."

Matte Glaze

A nonreflective glaze with no gloss as opposed to a gloss glaze that is reflective and shiny.

Onion Soup Bowl

A lug-handled soup bowl that has a cover.

Overglaze Decoration

Decoration applied after the glaze has been fired. This is done when the colors used to make the design would be destroyed in the kiln during the intense heat of the glaze

Lug Handles

firing. Overglaze decoration is usually made permanent by a firing at a somewhat lower temperature.

Print and Fill or Print and Paint
A technique in which the outline of the design is transfer printed on the ceramic and then the color is added by hand.

Redware
Earthenware made from clay with a high percentage of iron (ferrous oxide) in its chemical makeup. When this kind of clay is fired, it produces a finished ware that is red to reddish-brown in color.

Secondary Market
When an item is initially sold brand new to the consumer at retail, that is known as the "primary market." When an item is later sold to the collecting public, that is called the "secondary market." Primary market prices are generally set by manufacturers and retailers and have to do with the cost of making, marketing (advertising), and selling the item. Secondary market prices, however, are based on collector interest and rarity of the object in question and may have little relationship to the price it sold for on the primary market when it was new.

Semiporcelain
A ceramics industry marketing term that refers to pottery that is made from white clay that has been fired at a

Snack Plate

lower temperature than real porcelain and is not as hard or vitrified (i.e., glasslike). Items made from this are more porous than porcelain and chip easily.

Snack Plate
A plate with a raised circular rim near one end or side that is meant to hold a teacup. These are also called "party plates." These are specialty items meant to be used for entertaining guests and to hold a teacup, sandwiches, cake, and/or cookies.

Terra Cotta
An unglazed pottery generally made from the same kind of clay as redware. It is very soft and porous and unsuitable for making vessels that will hold water. When it is fired it is yellowish buff to red in color, and when a glaze is added it becomes redware.

Transfer Printing
Process first used in the 18th century as a cost-effective way to decorate large quantities of pottery and porcelain. It involved engraving a copper plate with the design that was to be transferred to the surface of the ceramic item being decorated. This required that a separate copper plate had to be made for each type of item on which it was to be used because the design applied to the plate, for example, would not fit or be positioned correctly on the jug or vase. After the copper plate was made, it was inked with an oily ceramic pigment, and after the excess was wiped off, the design was transferred or printed onto

Transfer Printing

a piece of paper. Next, the paper was trimmed, applied to the surface of the piece being decorated, and then soaked off leaving the design behind. The piece was then fired to vaporize the oil in the pigment and make the design permanent. Finally, the piece was glazed and fired again.

Underglaze Decoration
Decoration applied to the "biscuit" or once-fired ceramic body before the glaze is put on. Colors used in this type of decoration must be able to withstand the intense heat of the glaze or "glost" firing. Glost firing refers to the process of firing the glaze on a piece of pottery or porcelain. This is generally done at a lower temperature and for a shorter time than the first or biscuit firing.

Vitrified
Refers to an item made from clay becoming non-porous when it is heated to a high temperature over a period of time. True hard-paste porcelain is vitrified;

semiporcelain and most other earthenwares and soft-paste porcelains are not.

Issues of Condition

There are many factors that affect the value of a piece of American dinnerware. Shape, color, pattern, and manufacturer have already been discussed briefly, but there is another element that can be devastating to the monetary and aesthetic worth of any item: condition.

Collectors will sometimes forgive a condition problem if the piece cannot be found in a pristine, undamaged state. Enthusiasts are often willing to buy one-of-a-kind or very rare items with a chip, a crack, or some other problem if they know they are never going to find a better example.

As a general rule, the collector will purchase the imperfect rare example to fill a spot in a collection, but there is always the hope that the perfect piece will turn up and the "wounded" specimen can be retired or sold. However, with mass-produced American dinnerware, perfect examples are almost always available, and there are very few cases where a piece in perfect condition cannot be found somewhere at some price.

As we have said, collectors are sometimes willing to buy imperfect pieces if they are rare and not available in better condition, but some collectors will buy imperfect examples that can be displayed in such a way that the damage is not immediately apparent to the casual observer. In other words, a chipped "Fiesta" plate or a cracked "Autumn Leaf" cup is not necessarily a complete loss, but the value has been reduced by at least 60 to 80 percent.

Contrary to what one might expect, it should be understood that not all damage is created equal. In many instances, a collector would prefer a chip to a crack because a chip is a tragedy that has happened and is over with, while a crack is a disaster that is in progress and not yet completely over.

Unless a crack is professionally stabilized, it only gets bigger over time. Cracks are a bit like killer bees or fire ants—they creep forward into new territory little by little, bit by bit. Cracks are insidious killers of collectibles, and ceramics collectors hate them with good reason.

When enthusiasts talk about cracks, they are referring most often to the cracks that affect the body of the piece of pottery or porcelain, but there is another type of crack that affects the glaze. Called "crazing," these little surface fissures happen for various reasons.

Crazing can happen when the piece is being made and the glaze formula being used was not formulated correctly to accommodate the natural shrinkage of the pottery while it was being baked in the kiln. When the body shrinks too much, the glaze covering it must crack. But crazing can also happen after years of hard use when excessive heat and moisture cause these little networks of cracks to appear due to stress in the body of the ceramic.

It should be mentioned at this point that crazing is sometimes intentional and is meant to be a decorative element. When this type of surface is created on purpose, it is said to have a "crackle" or "craquelle" finish.

The Chinese developed this type of glaze treatment and invented a number of varieties to which they gave fanciful names, such as "crab's claw" and "fish roe." In many instances, the Chinese crackle pieces had ink rubbed into the cracks to emphasize their decorative nature. In American everyday dinnerware, purposeful crackle is seldom encountered, but the Dedham Pottery of Dedham, Massachusetts, did make some that is now considered to be "art pottery" and is highly desired by today's collectors.

Unintentional crazing is the bane of a collector's existence. It is sometimes forgiven when all the items in a line are crazed, and that is the only way they can be found. However, crazed examples are always devalued by at least 25 percent if there are pieces available that do not have these disfiguring glaze flaws.

Unfortunately, this devaluation is much greater when grease, dirt, and moisture have gotten under the glaze and caused the pottery body to become discolored and unattractive. When this happens, the unsightliness of the item makes it virtually worthless, and most serious collectors avoid these pieces more than they would one with a simple chip or crack because there is absolutely no way to display them or use them in an aesthetically pleasing manner.

American everyday dinnerware is often decorated with decals and overglaze designs that can be damaged by wear, and pieces with noticeable wear and fading of the colors are devalued by at least 50 percent. Still another type of damage associated with normal everyday wear is knife scratches on the surface, usually found only on plates and platters.

Sometimes platters are found that have such numerous and deep knife cuts that the surface of the piece resembles ice after a spirited hockey game. A few knife marks across the surface may constitute a 20 percent deduction, but a highly noticeable network of slashes may cause the value to drop by 50 to 75 percent or even more.

Fakes, Forgeries, Look-alikes, and Reissues

Currently, fakes and forgeries are not a big problem for collectors of American everyday dinnerware, but look-alikes and reissues can be troublesome for novices. Certainly some of the most vexing are the look-alikes of the famous "Autumn Leaf" pattern that many people assume was made only by the Hall China Company from 1933 to 1976 as premiums for the Jewel Tea Company. This, however, is not the case.

It is true that Hall was the only company that made "Autumn Leaf" pattern china for Jewel Tea, but the decal used was not an exclusive design and can be found on dinnerwares made by a number of other companies, including Crown Pottery, W. S. George, Columbia Chinaware (a division of the more famous Harker Pottery), Vernon Kilns, and Paden City. Indeed, as the cliché holds, imitation may be the sincerest form of flattery, but when it comes to collectibles, imitation can also be a major source of confusion and frustration for collectors.

Another pattern that was made by a number of companies is the one known as "Taverne" or "Silhouette." This design is most commonly associated with the Hall China Company and was made by them in the 1930s and 1940s as premiums for the Cook Coffee Company.

In addition to Hall, Harker Pottery and Taylor, Smith and Taylor made pieces with the silhouetted design of two men in colonial-style dress seated opposite one another on high-back benches with a table in between. One of the gentlemen is shown eating with a fork in his hand; the other is smoking a long-stemmed pipe.

The Crooksville China Company of Crooksville, Ohio, made pieces with a very similar design, except the two figures are sitting in chairs (one source suggests that one of these figures may be a woman, but careful examination raises some doubt about this conclusion). There is also a mug on the table, one gentleman is eating while the other is doing nothing that is discernible, and an expectant-looking dog sits on the floor between them.

These can be a little confusing at first glance, but a careful inspection and a quick look at the marks that are found almost inevitably on the back should clear up any confusion. Perhaps it should be mentioned that several companies made other patterns featuring silhouetted designs, including Harker's "Colonial Lady" and Taylor, Smith and Taylor's "Stagecoach."

Still another style of dinnerware that might cause confusion is W. S. George's "Mexi-Lido" and "Mexi-Gren," Paden City's "Patio," Homer Laughlin's "Conchita," and the Limoges China Company's "Old Mexico." All of these patterns include pieces of pottery placed in outdoor settings that look very "old world" or "Mexican," and at first glance, the various different patterns can be confusing to novice collectors.

Some forms of American everyday dinnerware are so popular with the public that they have been reissued in relatively recent times. These come in basically two forms: reproductions of early forms and entirely new items made in the style of the earlier product.

Hall, for example, made some reproduction Jewel Tea "Autumn Leaf" pattern pieces and some entirely new items for the Autumn Leaf Collectors Club starting about 1984. The first piece was a teapot, but subsequently there was a cozy set (also called a "tea for two" set), a round covered casserole, a vase, two kinds of candlesticks, a three-piece tea set, a chocolate cup, a "Baby Ball Jug," a "French" style teapot, a punch bowl set, a "Doughnut" teapot, an oyster cup, and a sugar or artificial sweetener holder, among others.

These are plainly marked, as are the "Autumn Leaf" pieces that have been made by Hall for China Specialties of Strongville, Ohio, since 1990. The idea was to release in limited edition pieces with the "Autumn Leaf" design that had never been produced by Hall during the original production period.

These pieces are marked with the Hall backstamp plus a date in most instances, and in some cases, the phrase "China Specialties Exclusive." Initially, the pieces carried a gold starburst-style sticker that says "Limited Edition Produced Exclusively for China Specialties," but often, these labels are removed after purchase. Reportedly, these have been well received on the collectors' market, and prices have escalated far above the issue price in many cases.

"Fiesta," by the Homer Laughlin Company of Newell, West Virginia, is perhaps the most successful of all the American dinnerware lines. Inspired by 1930s California dinnerware lines made by both J. A. Bauer ("Ring," 1931) and Gladding, McBean & Company ("El Patio," 1934), "Fiesta" was introduced in 1936 in shades of red (orange), cobalt blue, light green, yellow, and ivory (turquoise was added in 1937). By the late 1930s there were so many imitations of "Fiesta" (which is arguably an imitation itself) that Homer Laughlin had to start marking its pieces "Genuine Fiesta" in order to cut down on the confusion.

Since its introduction, new colors have been added to the "Fiesta" line from time to time. Starting in 1951, the company added rose, gray, forest green, and chartreuse. In 1959 one of the most sought-after shades was introduced—a Christmasy green that falls between light green and forest green, called "medium green."

Interestingly, pieces in these "fifties" colors are in many instances rarer than items in the earlier shades, and medium green remains one of the most sought-after colors by collectors. In 1986, to celebrate the 50th anniversary of "Fiesta," Homer Laughlin revitalized the line by introducing new colors, such as black, white, and apricot.

These recent reissues ushered in a collecting frenzy that is unprecedented in the annals of American everyday dinnerware. This new era of "Fiesta" has created some highly prized rarities; items with a lavender glaze, for example, can be quite hard to find and are somewhat valuable.

Analyzing the Marketplace: Where and How to Buy

It is possible to buy American everyday dinnerware almost anywhere. Homer Laughlin's "Fiesta," for example, is widely available brand new in a variety of department stores, in specialty shops, online, and in mail-order catalogs. Much the same thing might be said of "Autumn Leaf," although the availability is not nearly as ubiquitous as that of "Fiesta."

On occasion, new pieces of specific patterns are available through collectors' clubs that commission items to be made for their members, and it is always a good idea to join one of these associations if one is in existence. There are a number of these collectors' societies, and many can be found through a simple search on the Internet, but see also the section "Collectors' Clubs, Newsletters, and Web Sites" in chapter 4 of this book.

Buying American everyday dinnerware is something that can be done on the Internet using such sites as eBay.com, replacements.com, and robinsnest.com. These sites can make searching for a specific piece in a specific pattern very easy indeed.

There is no question that eBay has revolutionized the buying and selling of antiques and collectibles, and many thousands of pieces of American everyday dinnerware are available on this site at any given moment. EBay's search engines make finding specific patterns relatively easy, and shopping can be as simple as pointing, clicking, typing in some information, and waiting for your new treasure to arrive at your door.

Many collectors feel that the prices on some of the online sites that offer vintage dinnerware replacement can be excessive. But if someone is looking for a hard-to-find or rare item and it turns up on one of these sites, it can be a very exciting moment, and price is not necessarily as important as filling out a collection or finally completing a dinnerware service that has been painstakingly assembled piece by piece over many years of ardent searching.

Some people, however, are not comfortable with this on-line way of collecting and prefer more traditional methods, such as shopping at garage and estate sales, at auctions, and at antique shops and malls. Garage and estate tag sales are two of the primary places where fresh vintage merchandise enters the marketplace for the first time.

Prices at these venues can be attractive—if not downright cheap—and the finds can be very exciting. The major problem is that a collector may have to visit dozens of garage and/or estate tag sales before finding even one item to add to his or her collection. This can be frustrating in the extreme—but for many people, this search is itself both the essence and the fun of collecting.

Auctions are another place where American everyday dinnerware can be found at reasonable prices, although the competition of bidding can drive prices well above the level of those found at garage and estate tag sales. Currently, no auction house specializes in the sale of this type of product, and enthusiasts have to check each auction to see if particular pieces that interest them are being offered for sale.

Another drawback to buying at auction is that auction houses often do not understand American everyday dinnerware and tend to sell it in lots. These are either put together with similar items or grouped in a box with miscellany, which means that buyers often end up with items they do not want in order to get one or two pieces that they do. ◼

2

THE MAJOR MAKERS OF AMERICAN EVERYDAY DINNERWARE

There are hundreds of patterns available in American everyday dinnerware, but most of the ones that interest collectors were made by a relatively small number of manufacturers. What follows is the "top ten," or the predominate American dinnerware makers, in alphabetical order, with a brief history and a look at some of their more collectible products.

Before proceeding, a word about pricing. Prices quoted are "retail," or the value at which items should be insured. They are not prices at which the pieces that are listed with values can be sold. This is the "cash" or "fair market value," and it is generally 40 to 60 percent less than the price that is quoted.

Please keep in mind that the collectibles market is very volatile, and prices go up and down depending on a wide range of factors that relate directly to current collector interest. Also, prices vary from one region of the country to another, and all the prices that follow should be viewed only as ballpark figures that are intended to serve merely as a guide.

Gladding, McBean & Company

This company began operations in Lincoln, California, in 1875. The decision to locate this firm in this rather out-of-the-way location was due to pure serendipity that occurred when a decision was made to straighten an existing road by cutting through a low ridge.

Not ten feet into the project, the workmen struck a deposit of kaolin, and further investigation turned up other types of clay and coal. Charles Gladding of Chicago, Illinois, read about the discovery in a newspaper and traveled to California to investigate. He shipped samples of the newfound clay back to Chicago and to a friend in Akron, Ohio, who was in the business of making vitrified sewer pipe. The friend tested the clay and expressed the opinion that it would be perfect for making this type of product, and on May 1, 1875, the Gladding McBean Company was founded to do just that.

The principals in this new business were three friends, Charles Gladding, Peter McGill McBean, and George Chambers, and the first shipment of sewer pipe went to San Francisco in August 1875. It is said that the discovery of clay near Lincoln was more important to the development of California than the discovery of gold in 1849 because heavy clay building products no longer had to be shipped around the Horn of South America to reach the West Coast from the eastern United States.

The Gladding McBean Company began making architectural terra cotta in 1884, and in 1886 the company was incorporated as Gladding, McBean & Company. Over the years, Gladding, McBean acquired a number of other California potteries, including Tropico Pottery, Catalina Pottery, and the West Coast operations of the American

Encaustic Tiling Company of Zanesville, Ohio.

About 1932, Gladding, McBean began preparing themselves to start making dinnerware. At the time, three other California potteries were making solid color dinnerware, and after testing their products, Gladding, McBean decided these three companies were using an inferior pottery body that allowed crazing and was too fragile. They decided to use a sturdy, noncrazing body invented by Dr. Andrew Malinovsky in 1928, which contained talc rock, the same substance from which talcum powder is made.

One of the marks used on Gladding, McBean & Company's "Franciscan Ware."

The first dinnerware lines appeared in 1934. Gladding, McBean chose the trade name "Franciscan" to apply to a wide range of both art wares and dinnerwares because they felt this name symbolized California. Interestingly, these "Franciscan" wares are still being made to this day—only not in California.

Gladding, McBean merged with the Lock Joint Company in 1962 and became incorporated as the Interpace Corporation in 1963. In 1979, Gladding, McBean was sold to the famous Wedgwood Company of Barlaston, England. After the purchase, Wedgwood continued to manufacture "Franciscan" at Gladding, McBean's Glendale, California plant until 1984, when all operations were transferred to England and the California facilities were closed. "Franciscan" ware is still being made, but it is no longer "Made in the U.S.A.!"

The most important Gladding, McBean & Company "Franciscan" lines to collectors are:

"Apple"
This pattern with its raised apple motifs was first introduced in 1940 and was copied from the "Zona" pattern made by the Weller Pottery Company of Zanesville, Ohio. Pieces with lids have finials in the shape of apples. The decoration is embossed (raised) and is hand painted

Gladding, McBean & Company's "Franciscan" "Apple" platter, 14-inch, $75 to $100. Item courtesy of Kingston Pike Antique Mall, Knoxville, Tennessee.

under the glaze. A 10½-inch diameter dinner plate should be valued at $20 to $25, while the 9½-inch plate size sells for a bit more at $25 to $30. A cup and saucer is $25 to $30, a rimmed soup bowl is $25 to $30, and a sugar bowl and creamer set is $50 to $60. Hard-to-find items include:

14-inch diameter chop plate	*$200–$225*
19¼-inch oval serving platter	*$225–$275*
5½-inch wooden-based pepper mill	*$250–$300*
Large three-footed tureen	*$600–$750*
2½-quart casserole	*$450–$550*
Irish coffee mug	*$120–$140*

NOTE: All prices quoted for Gladding, McBean "Franciscan" dinnerware are for older pieces with American backstamps; pieces made in England with an English backstamp are later production and command less money in the secondary marketplace as a general rule. This particularly applies to pieces in the "Apple," "Ivy," and "Desert Rose" patterns, which are still being made.

"Coronado"

Also called "Swirl," this pattern was made between 1934 and 1954. "Coronado" came in a variety of colors in two glaze finishes. One group had a satin or matte surface, while the other was high-gloss or shiny. In the matte glaze there were shades of ivory, green, blue, white, gray, turquoise, and yellow. The high-gloss colors were turquoise, copper, coral, maroon, light yellow, apple green, ruby, and white. In general, the gloss colors of "Coronado" are the most highly desired by collectors and are harder to find than the pieces with a matte glaze. Of the shiny shades, coral is the least valuable at 25 to 30 percent less than the others. High-gloss copper, gray, and maroon are at the upper end, but the most desirable and most valuable are apple green, ruby, and white because these shiny glazes were available only as special orders. A 10½-inch dinner plate in turquoise matte is valued in the range of $20 to $25, but one in high-gloss ruby is $30 to $40. A cup and saucer is $12 to $15 in the matte glazes and in coral, but in rarer glaze colors it would be $18 to $25. Hard-to-find "Coronado" items include:

8-cup coffeepot, any color or glaze type	$125–$250
6-cup footed teapot, any color or glaze type	$125–$150
Covered casserole in coral	$110–$125

NOTE: There is a flat, nonfooted 6-cup "Coronado" teapot that should not be confused with the footed example. It is worth only about one-third to one-half the value of a piece that is footed.

"Desert Rose"

First made in 1941, "Desert Rose" is said to be one of the most popular patterns of American dinnerware ever made. This pattern features raised roses, and items with lids have finials in the shape of rosebuds. It should be kept in mind that both "Apple" and "Desert Rose" have been in continuous production since 1941. The popularity of these patterns means that there are vast quantities available and some pieces were made quite recently. A 10½-inch diameter dinner plate should be valued at between $20 and $30, a cup and saucer between $15 and $20, and a 6-inch diameter cereal bowl between $15 and $20. Hard-to-find items include:

6½-inch-tall pepper mill, bulbous base	$450–$550
2½-quart casserole	$650–$750
10-ounce Irish coffee mug	$160–$175
Tureen with lid	$700–$800

NOTE: The cylindrical "Desert Rose" pepper mills and the ones with a wooden top and bottom bring about 25 percent more.

"El Patio"

This was the first "Franciscan" dinnerware line made by Gladding, McBean & Company. It was introduced in 1934 and discontinued in 1953. Initially, this solid color ware was produced in just eight colors: white, golden glow, redwood, glacial blue, Mexican blue, Tahoe green, flame orange, and yellow. Eventually, however, it was made in either 19 or 20 shades (depending on what is being counted) and more than 100 different shapes. Rare colors in "El Patio" include celestial white, ruby, clear glaze, dark green, and black. Eggplant is also very hard to find and desirable. Pieces came in either a matte or a glossy finish, and for a very short time in 1935 and 1936, an offshoot called "El Patio Nuevo" was made. Like the original "El Patio," the "El Patio Nuevo" pieces were solid color wares, but they were two-toned, using one color on the interior and another on the exterior. Replacement value for a 10½-inch "El Patio" dinner plate is in the $15 to $25 range in common colors. Cups and saucers are usually valued in the $12 to $18 range, but one in eggplant glossy might fetch $30 to $40 and one in ruby $75 to $90. Hard-to-find items in "El Patio" include:

Coffee jug in metal frame with lid in black (Without the lid, the price of the coffee jug drops in half.)	$175–$225
9-quart punch bowl, common colors	$200–$275
Buffet supper tray with four removable inner dishes in various colors	$100–$150
13-inch diameter platter, eggplant	$70–$85
Carafe with wooden handle, red, glossy	$90–$125

"Fruit"

This Gladding, McBean line is on "Montecito" shapes and is decorated with bold decals of fruit and flowers. It is banded in dark blue with a lighter blue overglaze, and the fruit is rendered in blue to match the dark blue bands. There is a report that "Fruit" also was made in brown with a clear overglaze, but this variety is seldom if ever found. It was made in a limited number of pieces and was discontinued in 1942. A large 10½-inch diameter "Fruit" dinner plate is valued at between $15 and $20, and a cup and saucer is about the same. Hard-to-find items include:

14-inch round chop plate	$85–$125
13-inch octagonal platter with cut corners	$85–$125
56-ounce pitcher	$70–$85
6-cup teapot	$75–$90

"Ivy"

This is the third embossed line of the "Franciscan Classics" series, which also includes "Apple" and "Desert Rose." It was made initially in 1948 and is less well known than the other designs. A 10½-inch dinner plate is valued at between $25 and $35, and a cup and saucer is in the same range. Hard-to-find items include:

9-inch tureen	$400–$550
8-cup coffeepot	$225–$300
13-inch cake plate	$200–$250
18-inch oval platter	$250–$300
3½-by-4¼-inch oversized cup and saucer	$150–$185
12-ounce Irish coffee mug	$150–$175

"Metropolitan"

This line was created by Marc Sanders in 1940 for an exhibition held at New York City's Metropolitan Museum of Art. It was discontinued in 1942. The shapes for "Metropolitan" are basically either square or rectangular, and the standard color scheme was two-toned with matte ivory on the interior. On the exterior can be found satin (or matte) coral, turquoise, satin gray, mauve, or satin yellow. Solid color or monotone pieces can be found in matte ivory and shell pink buff, and this latter color is the rarest. The pieces exhibited at the Metropolitan Museum were decal decorated, but these never went into production. The "Metropolitan" shapes were reused from 1949 to 1954 in different monochromatic colors such as copper, hot chocolate, leaf, mustard, and stone. From 1954 to 1957, a three-leaf decal was used on "Metropolitan" shapes. The value of a "Metropolitan" 10½-inch dinner plate is $18 to $22 in a common color, and a teacup and saucer is $15 to $18. Hard-to-find pieces include:

6-cup coffeepot, common colors	$85–$100
6-cup teapot, common colors	$85–$100
Chop plate, aqua	$40–$50

"Montecito" and "Del Oro"

This solid color line was first introduced in 1937, and Gladding, McBean promoted it in their "Franciscan" advertising as a suave and formal line with beautiful contours and coloring. The initial color selection was eggplant gloss (maroon/purple), coral matte, turquoise gloss, celadon green matte, light yellow gloss, gray matte, and ivory matte. Later (around 1942) a gloss ruby (or Chinese red) was added, and it is by far the rarest of the "Montecito" colors and is valued at as much as four times the price of the other colors. The "Montecito" shapes were used for Gladding, McBean's "Del Oro" line, which came in two-toned shades of Chinese yellow and white. On a plate, the brilliant yellow was in the center with a band of white around the edge, which gives the impression of an intense sunrise. For a time, "Montecito" pieces were offered in two-toned varieties. The flatware remained just one color, but a cup may have one shade on the outside and another on the inside. There were four color combinations used on the hollowware—satin oatmeal and maroon gloss, satin coral and turquoise gloss, satin turquoise and coral gloss, and satin green and yellow gloss. Collectors need to be aware of these combinations because they may find a coffeepot with a satin coral body and a turquoise gloss lid, for example, and jump to the conclusion that the lid is a replacement, which would be a mistake. These duo-tone pieces are generally priced about 25 percent higher than the single-colored examples. Ruby is by far the most valuable solid color, and prices listed for pieces in the other shades should be multiplied by four when those items are found in ruby. In colors other than ruby, a 10½-inch dinner plate should be valued in the $20 to $30 range, and a cup and saucer is $25 to $45. Hard-to-find items include:

Red coffee jug with stopper and wooden handle	$130–$175
Turquoise coffee jug with stopper	$75–$90
"Del Oro" coffee jug with stopper	$85–$100
Turquoise gravy boat with attached underliner	$65–$75

14-inch chop plate eggplant	*$40–$55*
Red-footed tumbler	*$85–$100*
Duo-toned footed tumbler	*$35–$50*
Individual teapot (discontinued in 1939)	*$150–$200*

"Padua I" and "Padua II"

This was Gladding, McBean's first hand-painted line, and to make it they had to buy new machinery and hire more help. The new machinery was basically a turntable on which objects were placed to have circular lines painted on them with a paintbrush. "Padua I" had a clear overglaze on a cream- or buff-colored body that was decorated with concentric circles of brown and yellow with a stylized flower in the center of flatware pieces. Many of the new employees hired to paint "Padua" pieces were either art students or mothers who worked part-time while their children were in school. "Padua II" originated in 1939 and had the same hand-painted design as "Padua I." The only difference was that "Padua II" had a celadon green over-glaze instead of the clear one found on the original pieces. Both styles of "Padua" were carried by Barker Brothers Department Stores, which renamed the pattern "Freesia." Both patterns were made on "El Patio" shapes, but initially, "Padua" pieces were made in only a few of these forms. Many more shapes were added to the line in January 1942, but both "Padua I" and "Padua II" were discontinued later that same year. "Padua II" is much rarer than "Padua I." The replacement value of a "Padua I" 10½-inch dinner plate is $25 to $35, while a "Padua II" example is worth between $35 and $45. The 9½-inch luncheon plate, however, often is priced at $20 to $25 for both styles of "Padua." A "Padua I" cup and saucer is worth $20 to $25, while one in "Padua II" is $30 to $40. Hard-to-find items in "Padua I" and "Padua II" include:

12-inch chop plate, "Padua I"	*$110–$140*
12-inch chop plate, "Padua II"	*$125–$175*
Carafe, "Padua I"	*$100–$125*

"Rancho"

Like every other maker of pottery in America, Gladding, McBean was hit hard by the Great Depression, but by 1937, they were showing a profit again. In April 1937, they purchased Catalina Pottery, which was a division of the

Santa Catalina Island Company. This firm made a prestigious line of art wares and dinnerwares, and Gladding, McBean acquired the right to use the Catalina Pottery name, its molds, and all existing inventory. After this acquisition, Gladding, McBean continued to make many of the old Catalina products, but in the case of the dinnerware, there was a difference. When Catalina had made its dinnerware, it had used a two-fire system that produced a product that was subject to damage, such as chipping and crazing. When the line was revamped by Gladding, McBean, they decided to use a one-fire process using the "Malinite" body. As was said earlier, this body has a high talc content and was invented in 1928 by Dr. Andrew Malinovsky for use in making tiles. The resulting dinnerware was much more durable and not subject to the previous problems. The dinnerware was named "Rancho" and was a solid color line that came in a large variety of shades. The Catalina colors used by Gladding, McBean on "Rancho" include dark blue, red, sand, red brown, turquoise, and green. Other colors introduced by Gladding, McBean include dark yellow, satin coral, coral gloss, transparent, petal green, and ivory white. Most pieces of "Ranch" are rather plain, and the flatware pieces tend to be coupe shaped. However, shell-shaped pieces, pieces with tab handles, gourd-shaped pieces, and pieces with numerous lobes like the petals on a daisy do exist. Examples of "Rancho" are generally marked with an ink-stamped "Catalina Rancho" or "Catalina Rancho Ware," both with patent numbers between the words "Catalina" and "Rancho." This line was discontinued in 1941. A 10 ½-inch diameter dinner plate should be valued at between $28 and $35, an 8½-inch salad plate or a 7½-inch dessert plate at between $15 and $20, and a 6½-inch bread and butter plate at between $10 and $15. A cup and saucer is $25 to $35. Hard-to-find items include:

C-24 teapot	$175–$250
12 ½-inch diameter chop plate	$70–$85
C-44 covered chowder bowl (shell shaped)	$110–$175
C-30 lidded pitcher	$100–$150

"Starburst"

This line was designed by George James and was first available in 1954. It was a transfer-printed pattern of stars in shades of aqua, green, and yellow on Gladding, McBean's "Eclipse" shapes. "Eclipse" was a very 1950s design as was the "Starburst" pattern itself. There were candleholders with arched tripod bases, casseroles with pinch grip handles on the lids, and a barrel-shaped canister set (flour, sugar, tea, and coffee) that is now very valuable. The flour canister alone, which doubled as a cookie jar, is now valued at between $350 and $450, while the sugar canister brings a bit less at between $325 and $375. Other Gladding, McBean transfer decorations on "Eclipse" shapes include "Oasis" (1955, blue and gray with stars and lines that form squares) and "Duet" (1956, two pink roses with gray stems that are crossed at the lower end). These patterns are priced between 10 and 20 percent less than "Starburst," with "Duet" being the least valuable. An 11-inch diameter plate in "Starburst" is worth between $18 and $22, but the 9½-inch luncheon plate is much rarer and is valued at between $40 and $45. The cup and saucer in this pattern is $12 to $15. Hard-to-find items include:

Small 7-ounce mug	$100–$125
Large mug	$85–$100
6-cup coffeepot	$200–$225
2½-quart covered round casserole	$150–$175
Vinegar and oil set	$200–$225

"Wildflower"

This is a very attractive pattern that features embossed (raised) depictions of mariposa lilies, California poppies, shooting stars, and desert lupine that have been hand colored in shades of yellow, red, blue, and green. This very short-lived line was introduced in 1942 and discontinued that same year. Pieces in this pattern are not often seen, and prices can be rather high. A 10½-inch dinner plate is valued in the $125 to $175 range, and a 9½-inch luncheon plate is $110 to $130. A regular cup and saucer is $85 to $125, while a jumbo cup and saucer is $200 to $250. Hard-to-find items include:

Covered vegetable or casserole	$800–$1,000
Water jug or pitcher	$400–$500
Creamer and sugar bowl with lid	$375–$450
14-inch diameter platter	$350–$400

Hall China Company

In 1903, Robert Hall bought the old East Liverpool Pottery Company of East Liverpool, Ohio, and renamed it the Hall China Company. At first, Hall continued to make the same semi-porcelain products that the original company had specialized in, but after Hall's death in 1904, his son began trying to develop a vitrified ceramic body that required only one firing for both the glaze and the pottery.

One of the marks of the Hall China Company used on their "Autumn Leaf" dinnerware made for the Jewel Tea Company.

The problem was finding a glaze that could withstand the intense heat of the bisque firing of the pottery. They also wanted the glaze not to contain lead, to be craze proof, and to be nonporous. A single-fire process had been used by the Chinese during the Ming dynasty, and Hall China finally managed to unlock the secret in 1911. They called it the "Secret Process," and it is reportedly still in use today.

During the early 20th century, Hall specialized in making such things as teapots and casseroles for use by institutions such as hotels, hospitals, and restaurants. Their cookware became very successful, and in 1919, they bought the old Goodwin Pottery plant in East Liverpool just to make decorated teapots. Hall launched a program to teach Americans how to properly brew tea using a Hall teapot, and soon the company became the world's largest manufacturer of this type of vessel.

Hall began making decal-decorated dinnerware and kitchenwares around 1931; these wares were available to the public from department stores, mass merchandisers, trading stamp stores, and companies that offered the dinnerware as premiums for buying their products. Hall is still in business and is an important name to many collectors. All of their teapots and dinnerware patterns are highly collectible, but the ones that follow are the most widely sought after:

"Autumn Leaf"

The Hall China Company first made this legendary pattern in 1933 as a premium for the Jewel Tea Company, which was headquartered in Barrington, Illinois, just a few miles northwest of Chicago. Most of the marks found on Hall's "Autumn Leaf" read "Tested and approved by Mary Dunbar Jewel Homemakers Institute." Mary Dunbar was the maiden name of Mrs. Mary Reed Hartson, who became known as the "Jewel Lady" after she began answering questions about home cooking from Jewel customers in 1925. The number of different items Hall made with the "Autumn Leaf" decal is truly mind-boggling, and every now and then, a previously unrecorded form will turn up. These can be rather valuable. It should be pointed out that the "Autumn Leaf" pattern can be found on everything from playing cards and cleanser cans to tablecloths and blankets, and collectors of the dinnerware are often interested in these ancillary items as well. "Autumn Leaf" was officially discontinued in 1978, but reissues and limited edition productions have been made. A 10-inch dinner plate is valued at $20 to $25 and a cup and saucer between $10 and $15. The

"Autumn Leaf" round warmer base fits the 8-cup drip percolator and was made between 1956 and 1960. It is worth $125 to $150. Item courtesy of Chris Paddleford.

"Autumn Leaf" round bud vase, $200 to $250. Item courtesy of Chris Paddleford.

list of hard-to-find and relatively valuable items is fairly long, but a few of these include:

1-pound butter dish, lid with a bud finial surrounded by rays, called a "bud-ray" lid	$3,000 plus
One-handled bean pot	$1,000–$1,200
Two-handled bean pot	$350–$400
1/4-pound butter dish with winged or "butterfly" finial on top	$1,800–$2,000
9 1/2-inch diameter cake stand with metal base	$600–$750
Electric coffeepot	$375–$425
Cookie jar, two styles, both	$350–$400
Open candy dish	$600–$700
1989 Collectors Club candlesticks, limited edition, pair	$275–$325

"Blue Bouquet"

This pattern features bouquets of flowers interspaced with latticework around the rims of flatware. A 10-inch dinner plate should be valued at $80 to $100, and a 9-inch luncheon plate is $50 to $60. A cup and saucer is $45 to $60. Hard-to-find items include:

Teapot and lid with infuser, Aladdin shape	$225–$275
1 1/2-quart round, covered casserole	$90–$100
11 1/2-inch oval platter	$70–$85

"Cameo Rose"

This is another dinnerware pattern that Hall made for the Jewel Tea Company. It was introduced in 1951 and continued to be offered until the early years of the 1970s. The pattern is a white rose surrounded by buds and leaves with a leaf and bud garland placed around the edges. It appears on Hall's "E" shaped pieces that also can be found with other designs, such as "Monticello" and "Mt. Vernon." A 10-inch "Cameo Rose" dinner plate has a value of $14 to $18, and a cup and saucer is about the same. Hard-to-find items include:

5-inch cream soup bowl	$85–$100
6 1/4-inch tab-handled soup or cereal bowl	$20–$30
Quarter-pound butter dish with "wings" or "butterfly" handle	$300–$400
Teapot with lid	$130–$150
Gravy boat and underliner	$50–$60

"Crocus"

Considered to be the most popular Hall pattern with an ivory-colored background, "Crocus" was first made in 1938. The design features bell-shaped flowers and leaves, and it was a popular premium for gas stations, tea companies (other than Jewel Tea), and stores. It was also sold at retail. This is one instance where the 10-inch plate is rather valuable at between $70 and $90 each. This is because the 9-inch style is much more common and sells for somewhat less in the $20 to $25 range. A cup and saucer is $35 to $40. Hard-to-find pieces include:

6-cup "Aladdin"-style teapot	$350–$500
Soup tureen with clover lid	$350–$450
One-handled bean pot	$425–$500
9-inch diameter round vegetable	$60–$75

"Fantasy"

Designed by Eva Zeisel, this unusual pattern consisted of a black abstract design (really, a black squiggly scribble) on a white background. An 11-inch dinner plate is $26 to $30, and a cup and saucer is $20 to $25. Hard-to-find items include:

11¾-inch round vegetable bowl	$70–$80
8¾-inch square vegetable bowl	$60–$75

"Hallcraft"

This line was designed by Eva Zeisel and was first made by Hall in either the late 1940s or early 1950s. It was distributed by the Midhurst China Sales Corporation of Los Angeles, California, and came decorated in a number of different patterns and decal designs. The shapes are typical 1950s modern shapes that are often associated with Zeisel's work of this period. Many of the "Hallcraft" pieces are found in solid white, but satin black and satin gray hollowware pieces were made. These include the salt and pepper, the after-dinner coffeepot and coffee cup and saucer, the 6-cup teapot, the 6-cup coffeepot, the gravy boat, the 12-ounce sugar bowl, and the 13-ounce creamer. Pieces of "Hallcraft" are clearly marked with a fancy "H C" monogram and "Hallcraft by Eva Zeisel Made in the U. S. A. by Hall China." In white, an 11-inch diameter dinner plate is valued at between $44 and $50, and a cup and saucer is $35 to $340. One of the most popular patterns found on "Hallcraft" is "Bouquet," which, as the name suggests, features a large, colorful bouquet of flowers in the center of the flatware. In "Bouquet," an 11-inch dinner plate is $35 to $40, and a cup and saucer is $20 to $25. Hard-to-find items in the "Hallcraft" with the "Bouquet" decoration are:

14-inch diameter salad bowl	$90–$110
1¼-quart covered casserole	$120–$145
Three-tier serving tray	$85–$100

NOTE: "Hallcraft" in other patterns is priced less, sometimes as much as 25 percent less.

"Orange Poppy" and "Red Poppy"

Hall first made "Orange Poppy" in 1933 for the American Tea Company to be used as premiums. The beautiful orange poppy decals were placed on Hall's "C" line shapes for the dinnerware pieces; this line was in production until the 1950s. The 9-inch dinner plate (there is no 10-inch plate recorded) is valued in the $22 to $25 range, and a cup and saucer is worth $40 to $45. The "Red Poppy" line was made for the Grand Union Company between the mid-1930s and the mid-1950s. Unlike "Orange Poppy," "Red Poppy" is on Hall's "D" shaped dinnerware items. A "Red Poppy" 10-inch diameter dinner plate is $60 to $75 (the three smallest sized plates in this line sell for less than $10 each), and a cup and saucer is $20 to $25. Hard-to-find items include:

10¼-inch oval bowl, "Red Poppy"	$225–$275
13-inch platter, "Red Poppy"	$70–$85
9⅝-inch pie serving plate, "Red Poppy"	$75–$100
Serving spoon, "Orange Poppy"	$125–$150
1½-quart casserole, "Orange Poppy"	$150–$175
One-handled bean pot, "Orange Poppy"	$200–$225
Donut-shaped teapot, "Orange Poppy"	$500–$600

"Taverne" or "Silhouette"

Pieces with this attractive design were used as premiums by the Cook Coffee Company as well as Hellick's Coffee and the Standard Coffee Company. As stated earlier, there are several look-alike patterns of which collectors should be aware. This dinnerware and its accessory pieces were available in the 1930s and 1940s. A 10-inch plate in this pattern is valued in the range of $45 to $60, while a cup and saucer normally retails somewhere between $25 and $35. Hard-to-find items include:

Coaster	*$40–$50*
6-inch tea tile	*$110–$125*
#3 ball-shaped jug	*$125–$150*
1³/₄-quart round casserole	*$170–$195*
8-cup coffeepot, "Five Band"	*$160–$175*

"Wildfire"

This pattern was produced as a premium for the Great American Tea Company and consists of an undulating garland of pink roses and green leaves entwined with a blue ribbon to form ovals around the rim of the flatware pieces. The background is white rather than Hall's usual ivory. An 11-inch dinner plate is valued at $25 to $30, and a cup and saucer is $23 to $28. Hard-to-find pieces include:

2¹/₄-quart casserole	*$100–$110*
4-cup teapot and lid	*$125–$145*
Gravy boat	*$45–$60*
13¹/₂-inch oval platter	*$45–$60*

Harker Pottery Company

Harker Pottery is an American rags to riches success story. In 1839, Benjamin Harker sold everything he owned and left England to make a new life in Ohio. He bought some land in East Liverpool and built a cabin. Harker had come to America intending to be a farmer, but near his primitive residence there was a hill of clay, which Harker mined and brought back, using a mule to pull the heavy load.

He reportedly sold the clay to James Bennett, who had come to East Liverpool just a few weeks after Harker. Bennett took the clay and started a small pottery, which is thought to be the first pottery ever established in what would become one of America's most important pottery-making centers.

Legend suggests that Harker decided that if Bennett could turn clay into pottery and make money, so could he. Bennett reportedly lent Harker some start-up money, and Harker built a beehive kiln in preparation for begin-

One of the marks used by the Harker Pottery Company on their "Cameoware" line.

ning the backbreaking work of making vessels out of clay. Besides mining the clay, Harker and his family had to grind it by hand, cull out the debris and rocks, shape the vessels, and cut the timber used to fire the kiln.

The first utilitarian wares made by Benjamin Harker went to market in 1840, and this established a family pottery business that would last until 1972. Unfortunately, Benjamin Harker Sr. died in 1844, and his two sons, Benjamin Jr. and George, took over and called the company the Etruria Pottery until around 1846.

At some point, no one is sure exactly when, Benjamin Jr. and George dissolved their partnership, and over the years, the two brothers formed various partnerships with other people to make pottery. George started the George S. Harker Pottery, and it is this firm that evolved into the Harker Pottery that today's collectors know.

In July 1889, the Harker Pottery was incorporated. It was located in East Liverpool until 1931 when fears of Ohio River floods motivated the company to move to the former Edward M. Knowles factory in Chester, West Virginia, which is located just across the Ohio River from East Liverpool.

It is said that Harker began marketing dinnerware in 1923 and made a wide variety of patterns before the Jeanette Glass Company bought them in 1972 and shut down the operations. Crock pot liners were made in the building until it burned down in 1975. Some of the more collectible Harker patterns are:

"Cameoware"

This ware was made using a process developed by George Bauer and first made at the Edwin M. Bennett Pottery in Baltimore around 1935. After Bennett closed in 1936, Bauer moved his process to Harker and "Cameoware" was added to the dinnerware line in 1941. "Cameoware" was basically an engobe process that initially used

a cloth-covered stamp to create a cameolike design on the surface of the dinnerware. After the stamp was applied to the surface, the piece was dipped in colored glaze. When the stamp was removed, the white slip below would show through the applied color, thus creating the design. Usually, "Cameoware" is found with blue or pink backgrounds, but yellow can be found and there are unconfirmed reports that black, apricot, and green may have been made as experiments. The most commonly found "Cameoware" design is called "Dainty Flower" and consists of a sprig with leaves and two, three, or more blossoms. Collectors sometimes refer to this pattern as "Cameo Rose." Another commonly encountered design was made for Montgomery Ward, but instead of being called "Cameoware" it was named "Carv-kraft." The pattern for "Carv-kraft" is called "White Rose," and the design consists of a single white rose with leaves on either side. Other designs that turn up from time to time on "Cameoware" include patterns of vines, pears, apples, maple leaves, tulips, and wheat. Children's dinnerware was made in "Cameoware" as well, and patterns of ducks, elephants balancing on a platform, teddy bears with balloons, and a dog or horse pull toy can be found. Most of the "Cameoware" dinner-

A number of companies made dinnerware with a petit point decal decoration. This version is by Harker and is on a **cake plate**, $25 to $35. Item courtesy of Kingston Pike Antique Mall, Knoxville, Tennessee.

ware items were made on either "Shell Ware" (a swirl design) or the basically square "Virginia" shapes, but they can also be found on "Zephyr" shapes. A 10½-inch diameter "Virginia" shape "Cameoware" plate is valued at $12 to $15, while a 9½-inch diameter plate in the "Shell Ware" line sells for a bit less at $8 to $12. A "Cameoware" cup and saucer retails in the $12 to $15 range in both "Virginia" and "Shell Ware" shapes. Most "Cameoware" pieces are relatively inexpensive. Hard-to-find pieces include:

9-inch diameter salad bowl with an apple, pear, maple leaf, or tulip design	$30–$40
3½-pint batter jug	$45–$60
Rolling pin	$150–$175
4-cup teapot, "White Rose"	$80–$100
8-inch round vegetable dish	$40–$50

"Colonial Lady," "Colonial Silhouette," "Early American Silhouette," or just "Silhouette"

First appearing in the early 1930s, these lines encompass a number of black silhouetted designs that are often found on Harker's "Nouvelle" and "Modern Age" shaped dinnerware. These decal decorations show a variety of scenes, many of which include a "colonial" lady—a "colonial" lady seated in front of a fireplace, a "colonial" lady seated at a candlestand with a "colonial" gentleman paying court, two "colonial" ladies at a piano, or a "colonial" lady in front of a rose trellis. Also, there were images of a gentleman and his horse among trees, and a couple on horseback under a tree. A 9-inch diameter dinner plate in a "Nouvelle" shape is valued in the range of $8 to $12, and a cup and saucer is in the same range. Hard-to-find pieces include:

Rolling pin	$125–$175
Set of three mixing bowls	$50–$65
Pie serving plate	$70–$80

"Engraved"

This dinnerware was made in the same manner as "Cameoware," but it is a later product and originated in the 1950's. It is speculated that Harker changed the name to give the appearance of offering a new product to the public. "Engraved" pieces can be found with background colors of butter yellow, celadon green, celeste blue, coral, and pink cocoa (beige). Some of the patterns are "Brown-Eyed Susan" (a scattering of white flowers with brown centers), "Cock-O-Morn" (a crowing rooster with flowers at his feet), "Coronet" (large triangular leaves forming a ring around the edge of flatware items), "Dogwood" (dogwood blossoms with twigs and small leaves), "Ivy Wreath" (white ivy leaves forming a garland), "Petit Fleurs" (a band of five-petal flowers), "Provincial" or "Provincial Tulip" (an interpretation of Pennsylvania Dutch designs), and "Star Lite" (similar to Gladding, McBean's "Starburst"). Of these patterns, the most highly sought after appear to be "Coronet," "Petit Fleurs," and "Provincial." A 10-inch dinner plate in the "Engraved" series should be valued at $17 to $25, and a cup and saucer at $18 to $26. Hard-to-find items include:

13½-inch oval platter	$42–$55
Round covered vegetable	$80–$95
7½-inch round covered casserole	$120–$140
10-inch oval divided vegetable bowl	$55–$70

"Pate-sur-Pate"

This is really a grouping of patterns all made using the same process. Classically, "pate-sur-pate" means "paste on paste" and is a technique in which semiliquid clay is carefully and painstakingly built up to make a slightly raised decoration on a ceramic surface. Collectors tend to associate "pate-sur-pate" with fine porcelains made in Europe, particularly the famous Minton factory in England. However, the "Pate-sur-Pate" dinnerware made by Harker did not use this expensive method. All Harker "Pate-sur-Pate" dinnerware starts with a piece that has an embossed decoration around the rim. The piece is first covered with a white glaze and then fired. Next, a colored glaze is applied over the top and wiped from the rim so that the white glaze below shows through and is surrounded by the contrasting color, leaving a white decoration on the raised parts, a colored ground in the center, and colored accents around the white decoration. Some of the "Pate-sur-Pate" designs are "Floral Band," which consists of an attractive band around the rim composed of stylized four- and five-petal flowers, leaves, and stems; "Gadroon Edge," which has a very simple raised gadroon pattern around the outer rim; and "Laurelton," which is a wreath of laurel leaves around the central well. Colors found on "Pate-sur-Pate" include aqua, beige, celadon green, teal, blue, and yellow. Pieces of Harker "Pate-sur-Pate" can be identified by the mark, which is circular with "Pate-sur-Pate Ware" written in the center with the word "Harker" above and "Pottery Est. 1840" below. "Laurelton" and "Gadroon Edge" are probably the most easily found patterns. Hard-to-find pieces include:

Coffeepot	$70–$85
14-inch oval platter	$55–$70
Covered vegetable	$65–$80
Chop plate	$70–$85

"Royal Gadroon"

This Harker shape originated in 1947 and is distinguished—as its name suggests—by its gadrooned edge. It was made in solid colors such as celadon (gray green), celeste (sky blue), charcoal (gray black), Chesterton (silver gray), Corinthian (teal green), pink cocoa (beige), Sun Valley (chartreuse), and chocolate brown. Examples of "Royal Gadroon" can be found marked with that name under a crowned shield, with "Sun Valley" in the case of the chartreuse pieces, or with "Chesterton Ware" for the silver gray items. Harker also used the "Chesterton" name on other items in shades of avocado, Wedgwood blue, pumpkin, and golden harvest. These were all solid colored wares, but "Royal Gadroon" shaped pieces often were decorated with decals such as "Ivy," "Bermuda" (blue leaves), "Bouquet" (floral grouping that includes roses and tulips), "Bridal Rose," "Magnolia," and "Sweetheart Rose." Of these, "Ivy" is the most commonly found. A "Royal Gadroon" 10¼-inch dinner plate should be valued at between $15 and $26, and a cup and saucer between $16 and $24. Hard-to-find items include:

Teapot and lid	$75–$95
16-inch oval platter	$70–$100
Covered vegetable bowl	$110–$145
Gravy boat and underliner	$50–$75

"White Clover"

This is the name given to dinnerware designed by famous industrial designer Russel Wright and manufactured by Harker. It was made using much the same process as Harker's earlier "Cameoware," and the pattern featured very sensuous and modern-looking long-stem clover against a solid color or speckled background. This was Wright's first line of dinnerware and was produced in 1951. It came in four colors—golden spice, meadow green, coral sand, and charcoal. "White Clover" is fairly hard to find, and the color that is most desired by collectors is charcoal, followed by meadow green. Sometimes, plates can be found without the clover decoration. A 10-inch diameter clover-decorated dinner plate in charcoal is valued at $25 to $35, while one with no decoration is a bit less at $18 to $25. A charcoal cup and saucer is $18 to $25, and one in golden spice is about the same. Some of the harder-to-find pieces are:

Divided vegetable dish	$125–$150
Covered casserole	$125–$150
Covered pitcher	$150–$175
7½-inch round vegetable dish	$30–$40

"Wood Song"

This lovely pattern came in two colors—honey brown and Sherwood green. Of these colors, pieces in honey brown are about 10 percent more valuable than comparable items in Sherwood green. This pattern is composed of engraved maple leaves scattered over the surface of the piece of dinnerware. Hollowware items with lids have twig-shaped handles. A 10-inch dinner plate should be valued between $17 and $20, and a cup and saucer between $22 and $26. Hard-to-find items include:

Gravy boat	$60–$70
13⅜-inch oval platter	$50–$60
8¾-inch round vegetable bowl	$40–$50

Homer Laughlin China Company

There is some disagreement about the exact origins of the Homer Laughlin China Company. Some say the company's first predecessor was established in the year 1869, when Homer Laughlin formed a partnership with Nathaniel Simms in East Liverpool, Ohio. Still others maintain it was in 1871, when Homer and his brother, Shakespeare Laughlin, built a small two-kiln pottery near the Ohio River in East Liverpool.

To complicate matters more, other sources say the year the two brothers started working together was 1874. Homer bought out Shakespeare's interest in the pottery in either 1877 or 1879 and continued to operate Laughlin Brothers Pottery until 1896, when the company was incorporated.

The next year, however, Homer Laughlin sold his company to William Erwin Wells and a group of Pittsburgh investors led by the Aaron family (Louis T., Marcus, and Charles). At this time, the company was renamed the Homer Laughlin China Company even though its namesake had liquidated his interest and was no longer involved in the enterprise.

The new owners began a program of expansion, and by 1903 there were three plants operating on the East Liverpool side of the Ohio River. Then, in 1906, a new plant was built across the Ohio River in Newell, West Virginia, and by 1929 there were a total of five Homer Laughlin manufacturing facilities in production in that location. When plant #8 opened in Newell in 1929, the last facility in East Liverpool was shut down. Today, the Homer Laughlin China Company still operates in this West Virginia town.

It has been said that the Homer Laughlin China Company produced as much as one-third of all the restaurant and home-use dinnerware made in the United States during the 20th century. This company made a great deal of pre-1930 dinnerware, but the Homer Laughlin products that most enthusiasts are interested in collecting were all made after 1930.

Post-1900 Homer Laughlin dinnerware often has a date code on it. From 1900 to 1910, pieces had a single number to designate the month (1 to 12), another number to signify the year (0 to 9), and still another number to indicate the particular plant in which the piece was made (1 to 3). Therefore, the number 382 would mean that the piece was manufactured in March 1908 in Homer Laughlin plant #2.

During the 1910 to 1920 period, the marking system was much the same except the year was a two-digit number and the plant designations were the same with the addition of "N" to designate plant #4, "N5" for plant #5, and "L" for the East End facility. Thus, the designation "4 13 N5" on the back of a piece means that it was made in April 1913 in plant #5.

From 1921 to 1930 the system was changed a bit, with the months indicated by letters of the alphabet, with January being "A," February being "B," and so on. The next two digits were the year and the next figure indicated the plant. Thus, "D 25 N" would indicate that the item was made in April 1925 in plant #4.

The system from 1931 to the 1940s was much the same except the plant designations changed a bit. Plant #4 was still "N," but #5 became "R," while plants 6 and 7 became "C" and plant #8 was "P." This means that "H 37 C" indicates the piece was made in August 1937 in either plant #6 or #7.

This dating code was continued for some time, but occasionally in later years, a plain, noncoded date (such as "1980") is found below the company's trademark. Among the more collectible Homer Laughlin dinnerware lines are:

"Americana"

This pattern is sometimes referred to as "Currier and Ives" because of the decoration and the mark found on the back, which gives the name of the scene depicted on the front plus the phrase "From Currier and Ives Prints Made in U. S. A. by Homer Laughlin." On the front are scenes in transfer-printed red (sometimes described as either "pink" or "maroon") that are based on Currier and Ives prints, including "Home Sweet Home" (house, trees, a stream, cattle) on the 10-inch dinner plate and "View of New York" on the regular cup and saucer. These pieces usually are accented with a band of leaves around

Homer Laughlin mark on "Georgian Eggshell" plate. Note the date code "C 44 N 5," which signifies that this particular example was manufactured in March ("C" is the third letter of the alphabet and stands for the third month of the year) 1944 in plant number 4 (identified as "N").

the edge of plates or around the lid on hollowware items that have lids. Some rare examples have wide gold bands on either side of the leaf band on flatware items. This pattern was made between 1949 and 1956 exclusively for Montgomery Ward and was available from their catalog. A 10-inch dinner plate in "Americana" is valued in the range of $40 to $50, and a regular cup and saucer is $30 to $38. Hard-to-find pieces include:

9-inch covered vegetable	*$145–$160*
15-inch platter	*$100–$120*
After-dinner cup and saucer ("View of San Francisco")	*$65–$75*
Serving plate with center handle	*$60–$70*

NOTE: There are other Homer Laughlin patterns known as "Currier and Ives." These have Currier and Ives type scenes in the center, but they are in colors other than in red, and there is no leaf border. Instead, the outer edge has either a wide or narrow green band or a wide blue band. There are also reports of examples with a gold-stamped filigree band. These pieces are somewhat less expensive than the "Americana" pieces, in some cases by a factor of one-half.

"Eggshell"

This name was given to a type of lightweight body with thin chinalike edges that Homer Laughlin made to appeal to the fine china market. It first appeared in 1937 and was made in four different shapes. The first was "Nautilus," which was followed by "Swing" in 1938, with "Theme" and "Georgian" arriving on the scene in 1940. Both the "Nautilus" and "Georgian" shapes were made in a body other than "Eggshell," but all the "Eggshell" pieces will be marked with the word "Eggshell" and the name of the particular type of shape, be it "Nautilus," "Theme," "Swing," or "Georgian." For the most part, the various forms of "Eggshell" are decorated with a variety of decals, including "Adobe," "Mexicana," "Prima

Donna," "Green Goddess," and "Briar Rose." A 10-inch dinner plate in all the "Eggshell" shapes is valued in the $12 to $18 range, and a cup and saucer in the neighborhood of $10 to $15. Hard-to-find pieces include:

"Eggshell Georgian" plate with a flower bouquet decal, worth approximately $12 to $18.

Egg cup, "Eggshell Georgian"	$30–$40
Casserole, "Eggshell Swing"	$60–$75
14-inch chop plate, "Eggshell Nautilus"	$25–$35

"Epicure"

This modern-looking pattern was introduced in 1953 and was designed by Don Schreckengost. It is a solid color line made in shades of charcoal, pink, turquoise, and white and can be distinguished by its thin angled rims. A 10-inch dinner plate is $18 to $22, and a cup and saucer is $23 to $28. Hard-to-find pieces include:

12³/₄-inch oval platter	$56–$65
Coffeepot	$110–$145
Gravy boat and underliner	$60–$70
Two-tier tidbit server	$65–$75

"Fiesta"

Brightly colored to chase away the dark days of the Depression era—at least at the dinner table—"Fiesta" was designed by Frederick Hurten Reed, a famous English-born ceramist and former art director at Zanesville, Ohio's Roseville Pottery Company. "Fiesta," with its streamlined earthenware shapes and modern feel, was introduced at the 1936 Pittsburgh Pottery and Glass Show and initially came in colors of red (orange), cobalt blue, light green, ivory, and yellow. Turquoise was added in 1937. The red glaze was made using depleted uranium oxide and was discontinued when the United States government began the Manhattan Project during World War II and did not allow Homer Laughlin access to this raw material because it was being used to develop and make the atomic bomb—not, as has been widely reported, because the color was mildly radioactive and perceived to be a threat to the consumer's health and safety. In fact, in 1959 uranium oxide was made available to Homer Laughlin once again, and the manufacturing of the harmlessly radioactive red color was resumed. In 1951, light green, ivory, and cobalt blue were dropped from the "Fiesta" line, and forest green, rose, gray, and chartreuse were added. These are now called the "fifties colors" by collectors. In 1959, medium green was added, red returned to the lineup, and rose, gray, forest green, and chartreuse were discontinued. Currently, the most popular "Fiesta" colors for collectors are medium green, cobalt blue, and "radioactive" red, with ivory gaining ground. In 1969, "Fiesta" was redesigned and renamed "Fiesta Ironstone." This line was manufactured in only three colors—mango red (a nonradioactive red that replaced the original shade), turf green, and antique gold. "Fiesta Ironstone" was discontinued in 1973. To commemorate the 50th anniversary of the introduction of "Fiesta," Homer Laughlin reissued the line in 1986 using new colors including white (1986), black (1986–1997), apricot (1986–1997), lilac (1993–1995), raspberry (1997), sapphire (1997), juniper (2000–2001), sunshine yellow (2001), cinnabar (2001–), and tangerine (2003–). Currently, lilac, raspberry, sapphire, juniper, and sunflower yellow are the most sought-after colors made during the most recent production. It should be noted that these were limited production colors and there were only 500

(Top) Two of the original colors of Homer Laughlin's "Fiesta" ware were cobalt blue and red. **Cobalt blue soup bowl,** $50 to $65. **Red round vegetable,** $50 to $65. Items courtesy of Elaine Tomber Tindell.

(Left) In 1951, Homer Laughlin introduced four new colors to the "Fiesta" line: rose, forest green, gray, and chartreuse. **Forest green covered casserole,** $250 to $300. Rose **12½-inch platter,** $75 to $100. Items courtesy of Elaine Tomber Tindell.

raspberry pieces made (all bowls), and sunshine yellow was available on only one vase and one dinner plate, both of which were auctioned at the Homer Laughlin Collectors Association gathering in 2000. In ivory, a 10-inch "Fiesta" dinner plate is valued at $35 to $45, in red at $45 to $60, but in medium green the price jumps dramatically to $200 to $250. In post-1986 colors, a 10-inch dinner plate in lilac is worth between $70 and $85, and in

Medium green was added to the Laughlin "Fiesta" line in 1959 and is the most desired "Fiesta" color. **Medium green shaker,** $50 to $75. Item courtesy of Elaine Tomber Tindell.

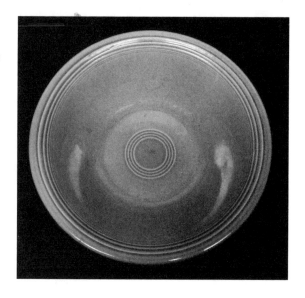

"Fiesta Ironstone" antique gold salad bowl, $45 to $60. Item courtesy of Elaine Tomber Tindell.

black between $15 and $25. In turquoise, a cup and saucer is worth approximately $35 to $45, and in medium green between $65 and $80. In the post-1986 pieces, a teacup and saucer is valued at $15 to $20 in apricot, and at $35 to $50 in sapphire. Hard-to-find pieces include:

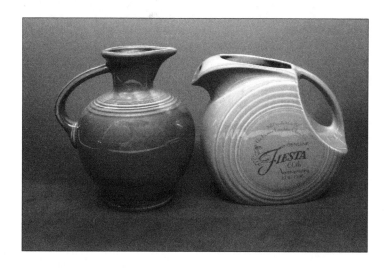

Coffee server, post-1986 chartreuse	$900–$1,000
Tripod candleholders, pair, red	$600–$750
Covered onion soup, turquoise	$8,000–$9,500
Covered onion soup, red	$800–$950
Cake plate, red, cobalt blue, or ivory	$900–$1,000
Juice tumbler, chartreuse	$450–$550
Juice tumbler, red, cobalt, or ivory	$45–$60
8-inch vase, red	$800–$900
11-inch diameter footed salad bowl, red	$650–$750
11¾-inch chop plate, lilac	$150–$200
4¾-inch fruit bowl, medium green	$450–$550

"Fiesta" pieces made after 1986 are very popular with collectors, and two of the most desired colors are lilac and sapphire. This **"50th Anniversary" disk pitcher in lilac** has four tumblers (not pictured) and the set is worth $100 to $150. The Sapphire blue carafe was a Bloomingdale's exclusive and is now valued at $40 to $60. Items courtesy of Elaine Tomber Tindell.

"Harlequin"

Introduced two years after "Fiesta," "Harlequin" was an inexpensive alternative that was made on a lighter body and sold only at F. W. Woolworth's. Like "Fiesta," "Harlequin" was designed by Frederick Rhead, and its major design element was concentric rings on streamlined Art Deco–inspired shapes. Unlike "Fiesta," the handles on "Harlequin" items are triangular rather than circular. "Harlequin" came in a variety of solid colors with the four original shades being maroon, blue, yellow, and spruce green. Later, it was made in chartreuse, medium green, light green, gray, forest green, rose, red, and turquoise. "Harlequin" was discontinued in 1964 but was reissued in 1979 for Woolworth's 100th anniversary

Homer Laughlin "Harlequin" teapot, $90 to $125. Item courtesy of Elaine Tomber Tindell.

as "Harlequin Ironstone." These reissued pieces were made only in turquoise or yellow and were marked with the Homer Laughlin mark, whereas the original "Harlequin" pieces were not marked at all. The most desired color in "Harlequin" is medium green, followed by blue, chartreuse, gray, dark green, and spruce green. A 10-inch dinner plate in rose (also called "salmon") is $40 to $50, and a teacup and saucer is $15 to $25. Hard-to-find items include:

Casserole with lid	$150–$175
Marmalade	$250–$300
Candleholders, pair	$275–$325
Demitasse cup and saucer, light green	$120–$140
Demitasse cup and saucer, maroon	$140–$160
Demitasse cup and saucer, mauve/blue	$80–$100

"Highland Plaid"

This colorful plaid design came in at least four different color schemes—brown and yellow, monotone green, green and black, and green and brown (called "Dundee Plaid"). This is a dura-print line and can be found on both "Charm House" and "Rhythm" shapes. Only the flatware pieces had the plaid design; hollowware items such as the gravy boat, cup, creamer, sugar bowl, and teapot were all solid colors. A 10-inch dinner plate with "Highland Plaid" is worth between $20 and $25, while a cup and saucer is $18 to $22. Hard-to-find pieces include:

Teapot	$50–$65
13-inch platter	$40–$50
9-inch round vegetable	$30–$40

"Historical America"

This pattern was based on the artwork of Joseph Boggs Beale and is most commonly found in red (or maroon), but it was also made in blue. This line has a floral border and was made from 1939 to 1958. Pieces are found marked "Historical America" with the name of the scene, and some are marked "Picture Reproduced From Original Painting by Joseph Boggs Beale." Scenes include such things as the "Pony Express" on the round vegetable bowl, "Ponce de Leon Discovers Florida" on the soup bowl, "George Washington Taking Command of the Army" on the 10-inch dinner plate, "Franklin's Experiment, 1752" on the cup, and "Arrival of the Mayflower, 1607" on the saucer. The 10-inch dinner plate in this pattern is worth $42 to $55, and the cup and saucer $30 to $40. Hard-to-find pieces include:

Teapot	$200–$250
13¾-inch platter	$65–$85
Casserole	$100–$125

"Jubilee"

This pattern was introduced in 1948 to celebrate the 75th anniversary of the Homer Laughlin Company. It was designed by Don Schreckengost and initially came in solid colors of celadon green, cream beige, mist gray, and shell pink. In 1952, "Suntone" was added, which had a brown (terra cotta) body with white finials and handles, a white foot on the eggcup, and a white underliner for the gravy boat. "Skytone" was the same type ware as "Suntone" except it was made in blue and white. Occasionally, "Jubilee" pieces were decorated with decals such as "Flame Flower" and "Stardust." These pieces are on the low end of the price scale for "Jubilee." Items in this grouping were marked both "Jubilee by Homer Laughlin U. S. A." and "Skytone by Homer Laughlin U. S. A." A 10-inch dinner plate is $12 to $20, and a cup and saucer is $15 to $22. Hard-to-find pieces include:

| *Disk jug ("Fiesta" shape)* | $250–$325 |
| *Covered vegetable* | $60–$80 |

| Coffeepot | $45–$60 |
| Juice tumbler | $90–$110 |

"Maxicana," "Mexicana," "Hacienda," and "Conchita"

Over the years, Homer Laughlin used a number of Mexican-themed decals to decorate its various shapes of dinnerware. "Maxicana" depicts pieces of pottery, a cactus, and a man resting under a sombrero (that's "Max"); "Mexicana" is a similar scene but there is no "Max" and no cactus, just pottery on the ground and plants. "Hacienda" features a bench in front of an adobe-style house with pottery on the ground and hanging on the walls, and there is a sombrero on the bench that suggests that "Max" might live here. "Conchita" depicts a string of hanging fruit and vegetables with pottery on the ground—one piece with a plant in it and another with flowers. These decals often are found on Laughlin's "Century" and "Eggshell" shapes. They are popular with collectors, and a 10-inch dinner plate is $60 to $70 while a cup and saucer is $35 to $45. Hard-to-find pieces include:

1-pound square butter dish	$150–$200
9-inch oval vegetable dish	$70–$90
Covered rectangular vegetable bowl	$140–$200
Cream soup cup	$75–$90
Batter jug	$150–$200

"Riviera"

Introduced in 1938 and discontinued in 1950, "Riviera" was the name given to yet another solid color dinnerware made by Homer Laughlin. Like "Harlequin," it was not marked. It was made to be retailed by the Murphy Company in their chain of five-and-ten-cent stores located around the country. "Riviera" shapes are based largely on Laughlin's "Century" shapes, which were used to make other lines with decal decorations, such as "Maxicana, "Conchita," and "Hacienda." The "Century" shapes are generally square or rectangular with square handles, and the plates, platters, and saucers have scalloped corners. "Riviera" colors are blue, light green, red, yellow, and ivory. On rare occasions, dark cobalt blue or rust brown pieces will turn up, but these were not part of the regular line. A 10-inch dinner plate is worth between

$60 and $70, while a cup and saucer is $25 to $35. Hard-to-find items include:

Demitasse cup and saucer	$85–$100
Casserole	$125–$175
Footed cream soup and saucer, ivory	$80–$100
Mug	$80–$100

Three 7-inch plates in the "Century" shape from Homer Laughlin's "Riviera" line, $15 to $20 each. Items courtesy of Elaine Tomber Tindell.

"Virginia Rose"

This is really the name of a Homer Laughlin shape that was decorated with as many as 150 different decal designs. Collectors, however, tend to associate the name "Virginia Rose" with two specific patterns, both of which feature wild rose decals. The first of these is "JJ59," which was reportedly made for the J. J. Newberry stores and has small pink and white flowers accented with green, gray, and brown leaves. The other design is "VR128," which is thought to have been made in vast quantities for Woolworth's. This design consists of both large and small flowers in shades of pink, white, and purple accented with green leaves with a hint of yellow. "Virginia Rose" was first made in 1933 and was discontinued in the late 1950s. A 10-inch diameter dinner plate with ei-

ther the "JJ59" or "VR128" decal is valued in the $12 to $18 range, and a cup and saucer $10 to $15. With other decals, the "Virginia Rose" tends to bring as much as one-third less. Hard-to-find pieces include:

Eggcup	$35–$50
Casserole	$85–$110
Cake plate	$50–$65

"Willow"

Usually known to collectors as "Blue Willow" because it was made most often using a blue and white color scheme, this pattern and its many variations have been around since the late 18th century. Typically, the "Willow" pattern features a prominent willow tree (thus the name), an arched bridge over a body of water, pagoda-like buildings, a pair of birds resembling doves, and Asian figures. These figures may be on the bridge, near the bridge, or on the water in boats. It is very loosely based on Chinese designs that are often associated with the port of Canton, but it is truly the invention of English merchants and Staffordshire potters who wanted to sell more dinnerware made in England. They invented this pattern with the sole intention of misleading consumers into thinking the motifs were Chinese, and they told buyers that the design represented a romantic legend from Chinese mythology. Supposedly, the "Blue Willow" pattern told the story of two lovers who were desperately fleeing from disapproving parents. As the lovers crossed the arched bridge, they prayed to the gods to be united forever, and in response, the gods turned the couple into

a pair of doves, which flew off together above the heads of the parents, who were chasing them. Despite the fact that this legend was a complete invention of the English merchants and potters, the pattern was so popular that it is still being made to this day. Homer Laughlin started making a version of the "Blue Willow" pattern in the 1920s, and initially, they decorated the pieces using a decal. These decals were usually small, and when placed on flatware items, they were located in the center of the piece with a lot of white space around the typical "Willow" image. Around 1936, Laughlin started making their "Willow" pattern dinnerware in the more traditional manner using transfer prints, which tended to cover most of the surface of the dinnerware items, including edges, rims, and the tops of handles. Homer Laughlin continued to make "Willow" until about 1964. It is important to keep in mind that dozens of companies in England, Japan, and the United States made "Blue Willow" style patterns, but Homer Laughlin's will be marked with the company name and the line name "Willow." It should be mentioned that Laughlin's "Willow" came in both blue and pink, with both colors valued at about the same price. A 10-inch dinner plate in Laughlin's "Willow" pattern is worth $20 to $30, and a cup and saucer $15 to $20. Hard-to-find pieces include:

The mark found on Homer Laughlin's "Rhythm" dinnerware.

13 ¾-inch oval platter	$50–$65
9 ¼-inch oval vegetable	$25–$35

Metlox Potteries

Metlox was founded in 1927 as the Metlox Manufacturing Company. Initially, they made large outdoor ceramic signs that could be fitted with neon tubing to make them literally glow in the dark. The name "Metlox" was derived from the phrase "metallic oxide," which was an important ingredient in the items being made. The plant was located in Manhattan Beach, California, and was owned by T. C. Prouty and his son, Willis.

The Proutys also owned a factory in Hermosa Beach, California, that made architectural tiles from Death Valley talc. Metlox specialized in making theater marquees such as the one on the famous Pantages Theater in Hollywood, and the company prospered in this trade until the Great Depression, when the demand for their products dwindled.

T. C. Prouty died in 1931, and his son decided to take Metlox in a different direction: the making of dinnerware. The first pattern, "California Pottery," appeared in 1932, and the "200 Series," which became known as the "Poppytrail" line (after the California state flower), was introduced in 1934.

One of the marks used by Metlox Potteries on their "Poppytrail" dinnerware lines. **This one is for "Antique Grape."**

World War II curtailed the production of Metlox dinnerware, and the company manufactured aircraft parts, shell casings, and nuts and bolts. For a time after the war, the company tried to make toys from surplus metal, but the red ink mounted up until the Proutys sold Metlox to Evan K. Shaw in 1946.

Shaw had the highly lucrative contract to manufacture Walt Disney ceramic figures in his American Pottery Company facility in Los Angeles. Vernon Kilns (see below) had transferred the contract to Shaw in 1942, and all went well until the American Pottery factory burned down in 1946. With the insurance money from this disaster, Shaw purchased Metlox from the Proutys in order to continue producing the Disney figures and to begin producing dinnerware on a grand scale.

Shaw hired the design team of Bob Allen and Mel Shaw, who had both worked in film animation and had designed the famous Howdy Doody puppet. Their first dinnerware line, "California Ivy," was introduced in 1946, and the decision was made to market it under the old Metlox name "Poppytrail."

In 1958, the owner of Vernon Kilns decided to leave the business and sold the right to use the Vernon Kilns trade name "Vernonware" to Shaw and Metlox. Along with the trade name came Vernon Kilns' dinnerware patterns and mold shapes.

Shaw set up a "Vernonware" division to compete with the "Poppytrail" division, and the two prospered until the early 1970s. Increased Japanese competition caused Metlox to begin to struggle, and the company finally closed its doors in May 1989.

Among the more collectible Metlox lines are:

"California Freeform," "California Mobile," and "California Contempora"

These three names refer to a trio of color schemes that are found on Metlox pieces that share the same distinctive shapes and decoration. The decoration looks like an abstract scribble that is said to resemble an Alexander Calder mobile. This decoration appears on the company's "Freeform" shape, which has a very 1950s modern feel with some serving pieces looking like boomerangs and others having oddly projecting triangular handles. The shape of the flatware (plates, etc.) is roughly square or rectangular with the points removed and rounded to create graceful forms that are almost oval. As might be expected from the design elements, these pieces were first introduced in the 1950s with "Freeform" and "Mobile" originating in 1954 and "Contempora" in 1955. "Freeform" features the abstract design in brown, chartreuse, and yellow against a pale gray background accented with flecks of color. "Mobile" has the same design in purple, yellow, turquoise, and pink on the same background as "Freeform." "Contempora" features the Calder mobile–inspired design in shades of pink, black, and gray with a textured color-flecked satin (matte) background or glaze. A 10-inch dinner plate is valued in the $35 to $45 range, while a cup and saucer is worth between $30 and $40. Hard-to-find pieces include:

Large salad bowl	$450–$550
Covered vegetable	$400–$475
Lid for the covered vegetable	$125–$150
Beverage server with a juice cup lid	$325–$400
12-inch round chop plate	$90–$110

NOTE: The "Freeform" shape was used for Metlox's "Aztec" line as well, but this squiggly line decoration in gray and black is a bit less desired by today's collectors than "California Freeform," "California Mobile," and "California Contempora." Prices for "Aztec" are at the low end of the scale listed above.

"California Ivy"

This was the first design created for Metlox by the design team of Bob Allen and Mel Shaw. It was innovative and modern feeling, and the plates and bowls were based on the coupe shape with a gently rolled-up edge without a pronounced or flattened rim. This pattern debuted in 1946 and remained in production until 1984. It was an unqualified success, and comedian Gracie Allen's picture graced the brochure, showing her with her "California Ivy" dinnerware at home. For this pattern, the ivy design was stamped on the items, and then the color was hand applied. The background was pure white, and the handles and finials were attractively formed to suggest vines. "California Ivy" was so popular that it was followed in 1949 by similar patterns named "California Apple" and "California Fruit." Current collectors, however, prefer the original "California Ivy," with "California Apple" and "California Fruit" commanding prices that are approximately 20 to 25 percent less. A 10-inch "California Ivy" dinner plate is worth about $18 to $22, while a cup and saucer brings about the same. Hard-to-find items include:

11-inch salad bowl	*$70–$85*
6-cup teapot	*$125–$150*
6-piece lazy Susan with metal frame	*$700–$850*
Eggcup	*$50–$65*

"California Peach Blossom"

First created in 1952 by Allen and Shaw, "California Peach Blossom" was the first of Metlox's sculptured patterns. Similar to embossed designs, this raised pattern was created by carving the design in the mold. Unlike many of the raised design patterns, the pink blossoms and brown twigs of this decoration did not go all around the rim but covered only a little more than half of the available circumference and left the rest of the rim bare. It is an artistic arrangement based on Asian designs and has a very "California Modern" feel to it. This pattern actually came in two varieties: "California Peach Blossom," which features blossoms in pink with yellow centers and brown twigs, and "California Golden Blossom," which was first made in 1953 and is the exact same pattern with green-centered yellow flowers and brown twigs. The flat-

Metlox "Peach Blossom" creamer, sugar bowl, and underplate. The underplate is very seldom found. The value of this set is approximately $85 to $100.

ware pieces in these groupings are primarily square and rectangular with some of the serving pieces being oval or 1950s freeform shapes. A 10-inch dinner plate is $18 to $22, but the 9-inch luncheon plate is somewhat more at $32 to $36. A cup and saucer is about the same price as the dinner plate. Hard-to-find pieces include:

Tumbler	$60–$75
Divided oval vegetable bowl	$45–$60
Coffeepot with lid	$150–$175
64-ounce pitcher	$90–$110

"Camellia"

This pattern originated in 1946 just a few months before Willis Prouty sold Metlox to Evan Shaw. It was a hand-decorated line with embossed decoration around the rim that was very reminiscent of such Gladding, McBean patterns as "Apple" and "Desert Rose." This one—as the name suggests—had pink camellia blossoms with stems and leaves encircling the edge of flatware pieces. These were placed against a cream-colored background, and the hollowware pieces with lids had camellia-shaped finials. This pattern came in two color schemes—one had brown trim and the other had green trim, with the green-trimmed pieces being about 25 percent more valuable than the brown-trimmed examples. "Camellia" was a great success for Metlox, and it continued to be made after the ownership change. A brown-trimmed "Camellia" 10-inch dinner plate should be valued in the $16 to $22 range, while the same plate with green trim is valued at $22 to $26. A brown-trimmed and a green-trimmed cup and saucer are about the same, at $20 to $24. Hard-to-find pieces include:

10-inch round vegetable dish, green	$44–$50
10-inch round vegetable dish, brown	$32–$40
13-inch round chop plate, green	$44–$50
13-inch round chop plate, brown	$30–$35

"Delphinium"

This is a very confusing pattern because it actually goes by two names. "Delphinium" was first made in 1942, and it was Metlox's first attempt to make dinnerware in the same manner as Gladding, McBean's successful lines that featured raised designs accented with hand coloring. The "Delphinium" design consisted of raised blossoms that were painted underglaze in shades of blue and pink against a background that came in one of three colors—blue, pink, or cream (plain). Unfortunately, World War II curtailed the production of this line, and when the making of dinnerware was resumed in 1946, the same design was used on a cream background with orange flowers and given the new name "Autumn Bloom." However, correctly or incorrectly, some collectors and retailers incorporate "Autumn Bloom" into the "Delphinium" grouping and list all colors under the latter name. A 10-inch dinner plate in all four pallets is $22 to $30, and a cup and saucer is about the same. Hard-to-find items include:

13-inch chop plate	$50–$65
Salt and pepper shaker set	$32–$40
10-inch vegetable bowl	$40–$50

"La Mancha"

This design is found on Metlox's "American Traditional" shapes, which are based on the configuration of 19th-century ironstone. The flatware pieces have a scalloped edge with a rim that is divided with raised lines. "La Mancha" was introduced in 1968 and came in shades of gold, green, and white. These solid colors were accented with two lines of dark charcoal brown around the edge with a thick line on the outside edge and a thinner line placed just inside that one. An unusual feature of this design is that only the salad plate has a bold dark charcoal flower-shaped medallion in the center that is supposed to bring to mind the legend of Don Quixote. In general, the prices for "La Mancha" green and gold are about 10 percent higher than the white. A 10¾-inch dinner plate is worth $15 to $18, and a cup and saucer is worth $12 to $15. Hard-to-find items include:

6-cup teapot	*$60–$75*
8-cup coffeepot	*$70–$85*
Divided rectangular vegetable	*$45–$65*

"Homestead"

This is one of nine Metlox patterns made using their "Provincial" shapes, which were inspired by American 19th-century items crafted from pewter, wood, tin, and rattan. The coffeepot, for example, was made to resemble a tin coffeepot with rivets down the side, and there was a dish shaped like a Victorian hen-on-the-nest with a basketweave base. "Homestead" is decorated with farm scenes rendered in the American folk art tradition with a stylized tulip border reminiscent of Pennsylvania Dutch design. "Homestead Provincial" used a dark green and burgundy color scheme, while "Colonial Heritage" is a similar pattern found in shades of red and brown, and "Provincial Blue" had the scenic decoration done in blue. "Provincial Blue" and "Homestead Provincial" were first made in 1950. Production of "Provincial Blue" ended in 1968, and "Homestead Provincial" was discontinued in 1981. "Colonial Heritage" was introduced in 1956. A 10-inch diameter dinner plate in one of the "Homestead" patterns should be valued in the $20 to $25 range, while a cup and saucer is about the same. Hard-to-find items include:

Turkey platter	*$350–$400*
Soup tureen and lid	*$700–$800*
11-inch salad bowl	*$100–$125*
Jam or mustard pot with lid	*$70–$85*
Carafe with lid	*$150–$175*

NOTE: Prices for "Colonial Heritage" are somewhat lower than for the other "Homestead" patterns, with a 10-inch dinner plate being worth $14 to $18 and a turkey platter $200 to $250.

"Pintoria"

Produced by Metlox for only a short period of time between 1937 and 1939, "Pintoria" is a very distinctive line of single-color dinnerware. There were only nine different shapes in this abbreviated grouping, and it is thought that it was meant to be a luncheon set. The flat shapes are rectangular with sleek, circular, dished-out centers, and the bowls and cups have very straight sides. "Pintoria" generally has a glossy glaze in shades of blue, yellow, orange, turquoise, cream, rust, or rose. Sometimes, pieces in pastel colors with a matte glaze can be found. The 10½-by-8½-inch dinner plate should be valued at $75 to $90, and a cup and saucer at the same price. Hard-to-find pieces include:

Vegetable dish	*$200–$250*
12½-by-10¾-inch serving plate	*$150–$200*

"Rooster"

This is the name collectors apply to three Metlox patterns that were made using the same "Provincial" shapes as "Homestead." The first is "California Provincial," which was introduced in 1950; next is "Red Rooster—Decorated," first made in 1955; last is "Red Rooster—Red," which originated in 1956. There is very little difference between these patterns, and all feature

Metlox "Provincial Blue" coffeepot showing the very distinctive "riveted" early American style shape, $100 to $125. Item courtesy Kingston Pike Antique Mall, Knoxville, Tennessee.

the image of a strutting rooster. "California Provincial" has a maple-colored background with the strutting rooster in maroon, leaf green, and straw yellow. The border is an undulating line with interspersed dots in green and coffee brown. "Red Rooster—Decorated" has the same bird in shades of red, yellow, charcoal brown, and leaf green on a textured white background with a smoky colored edge. "Red Rooster—Red" is much the same except some of the pieces are solid red—which Metlox called "live-coal red"—with no other decoration. There is also a fourth Metlox "Rooster" pattern that was introduced in 1966. Called "Rooster Bleu," it features the famous farmyard bird in pastel shades of blue, yellow, green, and orange with a flower and vine edge. A 10-inch dinner plate in one of the "Red Rooster" variations is valued at approximately $15 to $20, while a cup and saucer is worth $16 to $22. "Rooster Bleu" pieces typically sell for 20 to 25 percent less. Hard-to-find pieces include:

22¹/₂-inch turkey platter	*$275–$325*
11-inch salad bowl	*$85–$110*
Soup tureen and lid	*$450–$600*

1½-quart covered casserole	*$150–$175*
Three-compartment relish dish	*$125–$145*

"Sculptured Grape"

Found on Metlox's "Traditional" shapes, "Sculptured Grape" came out in 1963. It is an embossed pattern with raised grapes, leaves, and vines that is hand painted in shades of green, blue, and brown. The handles and finials are formed in imitation of grape vines. There were several variations on this pattern, including "Antique Grape," which was the same raised pattern decorated in beige against an off-white background; "Vintage Pink," again the same grape pattern but painted in shades of cranberry and chartreuse with soft brown vines; and "Grape Arbor," which is painted in various shades of green to simulate the types of grapes used to make white wine. A 10½-inch diameter dinner plate in both "Sculptured Grape" and "Antique Grape" is valued at $18 to $22. A cup and saucer in these two patterns is worth $16 to $20. These same pieces in "Vintage Pink" and "Grape Arbor" are 10 to 20 percent less. Hard-to-find pieces include:

6-cup teapot	*$125–$150*
1-quart covered vegetable and lid	*$85–$110*
64-ounce pitcher	*$100–$125*
12-inch salad bowl	*$80–$100*

NOTE: There is a microwaveable version of "Sculptured Grape" that is later than the original, which is not microwaveable; prices are comparable for both varieties.

"Shoreline"

This solid color dinnerware incorporated many of the shapes used for "California Peach Blossom" with the raised design removed and with some pieces redesigned to have a more modern shape. This grouping was introduced in 1953 with the intention of appealing to those interested in contemporary design, and the colors of deep sea green, driftwood brown, horizon blue, seafoam white, surf chartreuse, and wet sand beige reflected the popular hues of the day. Metlox decorated these "Shoreline" shapes with a distinctive leaf pattern in brown, green, and gold. When this design was placed on a white background, it was called "Central Park," but when the same decal was used on a beige background, the name was changed to "Indian Summer." These two decal lines are a bit less expensive than the solid colored "Shoreline." A 10½-inch "Shoreline" dinner plate is $18 to $25, and a cup and saucer is the same. Hard-to-find items include:

11-inch oval divided vegetable	$55–$65
13³/₈-inch oval platter	$50–$60
12-inch round chop plate	$50–$60

"Street Scene"

"Charming" is the only word to describe this pattern, which features various views of European streets lined with clusters of tall Victorian houses. These quaint domiciles are accented with various details such as street lamps, umbrella-shaded carts complete with vendors, horse-drawn wagons, and columned monuments enclosed with circular fences and trees. This pattern originated in 1956 and is on Metlox's "Confetti" shapes. A 10½-inch dinner plate is $18 to $22, and a cup and saucer is about the same. Hard-to-find items include:

13³/₈-inch round chop plate	$40–$50
Coffeepot	$125–$150
Covered vegetable	$80–$90

"200 Series," also known as "Poppy Trail" or "Plain"

This series of dinnerware originated in 1934 and was marked with the phrase "Poppy Trail"—two words not one as it was in later spellings. The name was derived from Evelyn White's book *California Poppy Trails*, which was about California's wildflowers. It is said that Willis Prouty wanted to re-create all the vivid colors of the state's wildflowers on this line of dinnerware, which was manufactured for approximately nine years. Initially, the "200 Series" came in seven gloss glaze colors—sea green, delphinium blue, old rose, canary yellow, poppy orange, ivory white, and turquoise blue. In 1935 and 1936, the coffee mug and the coffee jug were offered in glossy red, and these are the only items that were ever offered in this shade. Glossy cream and rust were added in 1937, but the original ivory white was discontinued. In 1938, matte or satin colors were added to this line, and these were opaline green, powder blue, petal pink, pastel yellow, satin turquoise, and peach. The final color, satin ivory, was added in 1940. The flatware in this grouping actually came in two styles. The flatware for table settings had rims, while the buffet flatware was coupe shaped and did not have rims. The prices of these flatware items are comparable in both the rim and coupe shapes. A 10-inch dinner plate should be valued at between $22 and $30, and a regular cup and saucer at $16 to $22. Jumbo cups and saucers are at least twice that figure, and the demitasse cup and saucer is about the same price. Hard-to-find items include:

Low coupe-shaped 17-inch salad bowl	$150–$175
2-quart casserole and lid	$115–$130
14-inch punch bowl	$175–$225
13¾-inch platter	$60–$75

"Vernon Della Robbia"

This is the name given to a Vernonware shape that was introduced in 1965. These shapes were decorated with an embossed design of a garland of fruit, flowers, and foliage reminiscent of the terra cotta work of the Florentine Della Robbia family, who worked during the Italian Renaissance. There were three variations on this embossed dinnerware: "Vernon Della Robbia," which was hand painted in brown, orange, green, and yellow against an antique white background (the company brochure said it took 531 strokes with the paintbrush to paint each piece); "Vernon Antiqua," the same embossed design accented with beige against the antique white background (first made in 1966); and "Vernon Florence," in which the embossed design was painted in blue, chartreuse yellow, green, and almond against a tinted white background. This ware was so popular with the public that it put the Metlox Vernonware division on a par with the Poppytrail division. A 10-inch diameter plate in one of these patterns is worth between $15 and $18, and a cup and saucer $15 to $20. Hard-to-find items include:

Teapot	$85–$110
12¼-inch divided oval vegetable	$60–$75
1½-quart casserole, round	$65–$80

"Yorkshire"

This pattern followed the "200 Series" in 1937 (some sources say 1936) and became a very good seller for Metlox. Supposedly, this swirled pattern was based on a 1700s English design, but it is also similar to Gladding, McBean's "Colorado." It is a solid color line that came in vivid gloss glazes of canary yellow, delphinium blue, old rose, poppy orange, rust, and turquoise blue. The matte glaze colors were opaline green, peach, pastel yellow, petal pink, powder blue, satin ivory, and satin turquoise. All the gloss colors were discontinued in 1941, and today, "Yorkshire" is known for its pastel shades rather than its vivid glossy glazes. A 10-inch "Yorkshire" dinner plate should be valued at $16 to $20, and a regular cup and saucer is $18 to $22. A demitasse cup and saucer is somewhat more valuable at $32 to $40. Hard-to-find items include:

Relish dish with five removable dishes	$85–$100
2-quart pitcher	$65–$80
13¾-inch oval platter	$50–$65

Red Wing Potteries

Deposits of clay were discovered near Red Wing, Minnesota, in 1861 by German immigrant Joseph Paul. Paul made some utilitarian stoneware pots from the clay, but he soon left the area. David Hallem began using the local clay to make stoneware pottery in his home in Red Wing in 1868, but this venture failed after a few years.

Then in 1878, a group of local investors organized the Red Wing Stoneware Company and made Hallem the manager. This company became one of the leading makers of stoneware in the United States, but by the late 19th century, it had competition from the Minnesota Stoneware Company (founded in Red Wing in 1883) and the Northstar Company (founded in 1892).

Northstar quickly went out of business, and in 1900 both Red Wing Stoneware and Minnesota Stoneware burned to the ground. Both companies rebuilt and in 1908 merged to become the Red Wing Union Stoneware Company, which stayed in business until 1967. Besides making crocks, churns, jugs, and other useful household items, thic company also made other types of pottery and began making decorative art wares around 1920.

One of the marks used by Red Wing Potteries.

In 1933, Red Wing began making art wares that were designed by George Rumrill, who owned Arkansas Products of Little Rock, Arkansas. This was a distribution firm, and these wares are marked "Rumrill" and not "Red Wing." Arkansas Products ended its relationship with Red Wing in 1938, but "Rumrill" pottery was made by other companies until George Rumrill died in 1942.

In 1935, Red Wing began making dinnerware. They changed their name to Red Wing Potteries one year later, in 1936. The first dinnerware lines were solid color wares similar to Homer Laughlin's "Fiesta," which did not originate until one year later, but Red Wings is best known for its handmade painted designs that were made until the company closed in 1967. Some of the most desired patterns are:

Red Wing Potteries' "Bob White" hors d'oeuvre server in the shape of a bobwhite. The back is pierced with small holes to hold toothpicks laden with tidbits. Originally priced at $4.25, it is now worth $75 to $95. Item courtesy of Kingston Pike Antique Mall, Knoxville, Tennessee.

"Bob White"

Introduced in 1956, "Bob White" was hand painted in shades of brown and turquoise on a beige background flecked with brown. Some pieces with an all-white background have been found. This was the most widely made Red Wing dinnerware pattern and is commonly available. "Bob White" items are found on Red Wing's "Casual" shapes. A 10-inch diameter dinner plate in the brown speckled background is $18 to $22, but with the experimental all-white background the price jumps to $150 to $200. A coffee cup and saucer is $15 to $20. Hard-to-find pieces include:

2-gallon water cooler and stand	*$700–$850*
Cookie jar	*$150–$200*
Tumbler	*$100–$125*
Mug	*$85–$100*
4-quart covered casserole with metal stand	*$140–$165*

"Flight"

A precise date for this rare Red Wing line of dinnerware is difficult to establish, but it probably was introduced in the early 1960s. This dating is based partially on the design being on Red Wing's "Cylinder" (or "Duo-Tone") shapes, which originated in 1962. This particular pattern is composed of black, brown, and beige ducks in flight over a sparsely stylized marsh background. A dinner plate in this line is worth $110 to $140, and a cup and saucer $65 to $85. Hard-to-find items include:

Divided vegetable dish	*$75–$100*
Covered gravy boat	*$90–$125*
1½-quart water pitcher	*$125–$150*

"Lexington" or "Lexington Rose"

Introduced in 1941, "Lexington" or "Lexington Rose" was a pattern that featured bold pink roses in full bloom with green leaves against a white background. It was made on Red Wing's "Casual" shapes, with flatware items having a squared coupe profile and rounded corners. A 10½-inch dinner plate is $15 to $18, and a coffee cup and saucer is $16 to $22. Hard-to-find items include:

13-inch oval platter	*$45–$60*
1¼-quart covered casserole	*$85–$100*
Egg plate with cover	*$200–$250*
Supper tray (three compartments with a cup holder)	*$28–$35*

"Plum Blossom"

Found on "Dynasty" shapes, this pattern was painted with either pink or yellow Asian-inspired flowers with brown stems and twigs. The flatware is hexagonal in shape with six deep notches around the edge. This pattern first appeared in 1949 and is the only design put on the very distinctive "Dynasty" forms. A 10½-inch dinner plate is $20 to $25, and a cup and saucer is $25 to $30. Hard-to-find items include:

13-inch oval platter	*$60–$75*
15-inch oval platter	*$90–$110*
Gravy boat	*$70–$85*

"Provincial"

"Provincial" is actually the name of a Red Wing shape that was introduced in 1941, and on these shapes, Red Wing produced their first hand-decorated dinnerware. There were four patterns. The most distinctive feature of "Brittany" is the large full-blown yellow rose that is located in the lower center surrounded by other flowers, leaves, and buds in yellow, blue, and green. "Orleans" is a very similar pattern with a big red rose in the lower center surrounded by multicolored flowers and green leaves.

"Normandy" is distinguished by a luscious red apple, green leaves, and white apple blossoms ("Normandy" also was available with a striped edge and a plain center). Finally, "Ardennes" has a wreath of green leaves around the outer edge. Early examples of "Ardennes" have the leaves against a white background; a later version had the leaves painted on a light green background. Of the four "Provincial" patterns, "Brittany" and "Orleans" are the most valuable, with "Normandy" close behind. An "Orleans" 10-inch dinner plate is valued in the $25 to $28 range; a "Brittany" example brings about the same. A "Normandy" dinner plate is worth a bit less at $20 to $24, and an "Ardennes" dinner plate is only about $15 to $20. An "Orleans" cup and saucer is $32 to $35, a set in "Brittany" is about the same, and one in "Normandy" is $24 to $28. An "Ardennes" cup and saucer is $18 to $22. Hard-to-find items include:

1-quart casserole, "Brittany"	$125–$150
Chop plate, "Brittany"	$65–$75
Gravy boat, "Normandy"	$80–$100
Candleholders, "Normandy"	$80–$100
Sugar bowl, "Orleans"	$60–$75
4-cup teapot, "Orleans"	$125–$150
48-ounce jug, "Orleans"	$85–$100

NOTE: Do not confuse Red Wing's "Provincial" shaped dinnerware discussed above with their "Provincial" dinnerware line that came out in 1963. This later dinnerware is distinguished by a red bittersweet solid color glaze.

"Reed"

This is the name of the solid color dinnerware introduced by Red Wing in 1935. It is a very simple pattern with a reeded band around the edge of plates and platters and around the body of cups. "Reed" was made in shades of ivory, orange, royal blue, turquoise, and yellow. Royal blue is the most sought-after color, and prices are about 25 percent higher than those for the other hues. A 9½-inch diameter dinner plate in "Reed" is $10 to $18, and a coffee cup and saucer is $12 to $25. However, a teacup and saucer is $20 to $35, and an after-dinner cup and saucer is $25 to $40. The difference between a coffee cup and a teacup is that the coffee cup is low and squatty, while the teacup is taller and has a fancier handle. The after-dinner cup is smaller than either one and has a fancy handle similar to the one on the teacup. Hard-to-find items include:

8-cup teapot	*$75–$100*
56-ounce covered batter pitcher	*$75–$100*
Covered toast dish	*$50–$75*
Three-compartment artichoke plate	*$30–$45*

"Round-Up"

Also on Red Wing's "Casual" shape dinnerware was "Round-Up," a hard-to-find pattern that features images of cowboys roping and branding. "Round-Up" was introduced in 1958, and a 10½-inch dinner plate with a "Chuckwagon" design generally retails between $70 and $85, while the same plate with cowboys around a campfire brings a bit more at $110 to $140. A coffee cup and saucer is worth between $50 and $65. Hard-to-find items include:

Cruet set on stand (two bottles)	*$500–$600*
24-inch tray	*$175–$225*
Covered gravy boat in metal stand	*$250–$300*
Quarter-pound butter dish	*$200–$250*

"Smart Set"

Distinguished by black and yellow geometric forms in squares and trapezoids on an off-white background, "Smart Set" was made on Red Wing's "Casual" shape. It was introduced in 1955, and many of the items—such as the cruet set, the teapot, the beverage server, and the various sizes of casseroles—had metal holders. When these pieces are found with their original metal accessories, this adds about 30 percent to the prices. A 10½-inch dinner plate is $30 to $40, and a cup and saucer is $35 to $45. Hard-to-find items include:

20-inch platter with metal stand	*$160–$200*
1-quart covered casserole	*$90–$110*
Lazy Susan with five sauce dishes and metal stand	*$200–$250*

"Tampico"

Introduced in 1955, "Tampico" is a hand-painted design that has an exotic look with hanging melons, scattered leaves, and a wicker-wrapped wine bottle. The background is lightly flecked with brown, and the design is ex-

Red Wing Potteries'"Capistrano" pattern dinnerware on their "Anniversary" shape. This very modernistic-shaped dinnerware has attractive swooping swallows hand painted on each piece; hollowware pieces have a sage green basketweave design on the exterior. First introduced in 1953, this is a delightful pattern that is still reasonably priced for collectors. Sugar bowl, $20 to $25 (creamer not pictured is the same), rectangular bread tray $35 to $50, and buffet bowl $35 to $50. Items courtesy of Kingston Pike Antique Mall, Knoxville, Tennessee.

ecuted in shades of browns, greens, and pinkish red. "Tampico" is on Red Wing's "Futura" shapes. A 10-inch diameter dinner plate is worth $30 to $40, and a cup and saucer is worth two to five dollars more. Hard-to-find pieces include:

Mug	$55–$65
Beverage server with lid	$100–$125
Footed cake plate	$100–$125
12-inch diameter salad bowl	$80–$100
3-cup teapot	$120–$150

"Town and Country"

This line was made for only one year, in 1947. Designed by Eva Zeisel, "Town and Country" is a solid color ware with very modern, irregular shapes. Handles are often off center or extensions of rims, and pitchers and jugs are ergonomically shaped to fit the human hand. This line is typically unmarked, but it is recognized by the unusual shape and distinctive glossy or half-matte colors of bronze (metallic brown or "gunmetal"), gray, rust, chalk white, chartreuse, coral, dusk blue, forest green, sand, peach, jade or Ming green, lime green, light blue, and plum or mulberry. In the late 1990s, Eva Zeisel gave permission for World of Ceramics to reissue some of the "Town and Country" shapes in colors other than the originals. A syrup pitcher, a mixing bowl, and salt and pepper shakers were made, all marked with the initials "EZ" and a two-numeral date, such as "EZ97." A 1947 10-inch diameter "Town and Country" dinner plate is valued in the $45 to $60 range, and a cup and saucer at $35 to $45. Hard-to-find pieces include:

Bean pot	*$250–$350*
13-inch diameter salad bowl	*$90–$125*
10-inch oval baker	*$100–$125*

Southern Potteries

Erwin, Tennessee, was the perfect place to build a pottery. The hills held the natural resources of kaolin and feldspar (petuntse), and there was a labor force eager for employment. During World War I, the Carolina, Clinchfield, and Ohio River Railroad sold land to E. J. Owen and his son Ted to build a pottery because the railroad needed industry along its route so it could transport the freight associated with this kind of manufacturing.

The pottery, originally named the "Clinchfield Pottery," opened in 1918, making fairly typical transfer-printed and gilded dinnerware. In 1920, the facility was incorporated as Southern Potteries. Unfortunately, the items the company made were not a resounding success, and in 1922, the Owens sold the facilities to Charles Foreman, who promptly revolutionized the product line.

Foreman utilized the large pool of unemployed mountain women in the vicinity of Erwin to hand paint designs on the dinnerware the company was making instead of using the standard transfer prints. These vibrant-colored, sometimes primitive designs offered an attractive alternative to the dinnerware that was available at the time, and Southern Potteries prospered.

This "hand-painted under the glaze" ware was sold under the trade name Blue Ridge and was most popular during the late 1930s, 1940s, and early 1950s. Much of it was sold by mass merchandisers, such as Sears and Montgomery Ward, but the company also sold dinnerware (mainly "seconds") to small rural customers out of the back of a pickup truck.

It is a bit hard to believe, but during its peak of production, Southern Potteries hand painted more than 300,000 items each week to keep up with demand. World War II contributed to the success of Southern Potteries because dinnerware imports from Japan and Germany were curtailed and "Blue Ridge" dinnerware helped fill the gap in a significant way.

"Blue Ridge" dinnerware came in 12 basic shapes—"Astor," "Candlewick," "Clinchfield," "Colonial," "Palisades," "Piecrust," "Skyline," "Skyline Studioware," "Trailway," "Trellis," "Waffle," and "Woodcrest"—and the various designs were painted on these basic shapes. The "Palisades," "Piecrust," "Skyline," "Trailway," and "Woodcrest" shapes were adopted later in the company's existence (post-1948), and they generally command about 25 to 35 percent less than the items with the earlier shapes.

This is at least partially due to the opinion held by many collectors that the hand-painted designs on these shapes are not as attractive or as well done as the patterns found on the earlier shapes. "Waffle" (also called "Monticello") and "Trellis" are very rare shape designs, and collectors only hope to find a few pieces in these patterns—finding a whole set is out of the question. "Waffle" can be recognized by its square wafflelike indentations around the outer rim, and "Trellis" has a crosshatched trellis design between fluted panels.

Beyond the consideration of shape, collectors are very interested in a number of the "Blue Ridge" painted designs, and at one time, Southern Potteries carried more than 400 different hand-painted patterns in open stock. At this point, it should be mentioned that artist-signed pieces of "Blue Ridge" dinnerware can sell for considerable amounts of money. An artist-signed "Turkey" pattern plate, for example, should be valued in the $800 to $950 range, and almost any artist-signed 10-inch dinner plate is worth $400 to $500. Most "Blue Ridge" artist-signed platters are now approaching the $1,500 to $1,800 level.

Floral patterns or designs with images of fruit are fairly common in "Blue Ridge" wares and can be found easily on the current market. A dinner plate with one of these common designs is usually valued in the $25 to $35 range, while a dinner plate with a more unusual pattern might fetch between $65 and $85 or a bit more.

Toward the end of their existence, Southern Potteries modified the way they "hand painted" their dinnerware. Stamps were used to apply a pattern to the china bodies, and the painters just colored in the designs the way a child would crayon in the pictures in a coloring book. Most collectors do not find these wares to be of great interest.

In the mid-1950s, Japanese and European competition was once again up to full strength, and Southern Potteries closed its doors in January 1957. "Blue Ridge" china is very popular with today's collectors, and some of the more desired patterns are decorated with portraits of people, square dancers, ships, roosters, landscapes, holiday themes, pixies, Mexican themes, or birds and other animals. Some of the most sought-after "Blue Ridge" dinnerware items tend to be in the following patterns:

"Chintz"

This is an elaborate floral pattern that consists of a profusion of posies and their stems strewn across the surface of the piece of dinnerware. The brown stems and green leaves seem to form a network that is dotted with blossoms in colors of red, pink, blue, and yellow (all of these colors may not appear on all pieces of "Chintz"). The centers of these flowers are often dark, but a yellow flower may be painted with a rich golden center or may have a center that is almost red. "Chintz" is a very popular pattern with collectors, and it is one in which dinnerware sets can be assembled with some ease. A "Chintz" dinner plate is valued at $65 to $75, a luncheon plate is $40 to $50, and a cup and saucer is $60 to $70. Hard-to-find pieces include:

Round open vegetable	$120–$145
12-inch chop plate	$180–$200
Gravy boat	$200–$225
Leaf-shaped dish with handle	$125–$150

"French Peasant"

Based on the famous French Quimper pieces, the flatware items in this line usually have the portrait of either a man or a woman dressed in Breton-style peasant clothing surrounded by a border of leaves and flowers. Larger pieces may have both the man and the woman depicted on them. On "French Peasant" pieces, the male figure is holding a whip shaped like a capital *R* while the female figure has on a white cap and holds a flower. There were many variations on this theme. These include "Brittany," which features similar male and female portraits with a border of red stylized leaves; "Lyonaise," which has similar figures and a bright yellow rim accented with black concentric rings; "Picardy," which is decorated with a wide pink border around the rim and has a European-looking couple in the center—he in a cloak with a feather in his cap and she in a pink dress with blue apron; and "Orleans," which has the couple in the center with simple branches and leaves and a wide multicolored border around the rim. A 10-inch dinner plate in "French Peasant" should be valued at between $85 and $120, and a regular cup and saucer is about the same. A demitasse cup and saucer is somewhat more valuable at between $175 and $225. Hard-to-find pieces include:

Demitasse pot, porcelain	$300–$400
Covered toast server	$375–$475
2-cup chocolate pot	$500–$600
15-inch serving platter	$300–$350

"Wild Strawberry"

This pattern is very simple, but very charming. Most pieces are painted with a single red strawberry surmounted by a triple-pointed green leaf that is as large as, or larger than, the strawberry itself. Sometimes, this leaf appears to be just one leaf, other times it appears to be three leaves. On larger flatware items, there may be two strawberries depicted, but this is not always the case. Pieces of "Wild Strawberry" are finished with a jagged border around rims and outer edges in green. A dinner plate in "Wild Strawberry" is $35 to $40, a luncheon plate is $20 to $25, and a cup and saucer is $35 to $40. Hard-to-find items include:

12-inch chop plate	$75–$90
Gravy boat	$80–$100
14-inch oval platter	$70–$85

NOTE: In the 1940s a Southern Potteries sales representative opened a small glass factory in Bowling Green,

Ohio. His decorators learned the painting techniques used by the women who embellished Blue Ridge china in the factory in Erwin, Tennessee, and the Bowling Green artists were able to turn out decorated glassware that matched Blue Ridge patterns. Later, undecorated glass blanks were bought from both Libby and Federal and decorated with Blue Ridge designs. Tumblers in various sizes are the most commonly found items, but pitchers, bowls, and sherbets also were made.

Stangl

Abraham Fulper worked for Samuel Hill making earthenware and drain tiles in Flemington, New Jersey, and when Hill died in 1858, Fulper bought the company and it became Fulper Pottery. Fulper expanded the company's operations to make both earthenware and stoneware and began manufacturing such useful items as vinegar jugs, butter churns, poultry fountains, bottles, and pickling jars. Fulper, however, is probably best known for its early 20th-century line of fine art pottery done in the American Arts and Crafts style. In 1910, Martin Stangl became Fulper's ceramics engineer and plant superintendent, but he left in 1914 to work for the Haeger Pottery in Dundee, Illinois. Stangl returned to Fulper in 1920 as general manager, and he became president of the company in 1928. The next year (1929), the old Fulper Pottery burned down and the company moved its operations to the site of the old Anchor Pottery Company in Trenton, New Jersey, which they had acquired in 1926. Fulper produced the first solid color (other than white) dinnerware made in America in 1920, but the only color available was green until the 1930s, when other hues were added. The mark "Stangl Pottery" was used on dinnerware as early as the late 1920s, but it was not officially adopted until 1955. The company closed in 1978. Stangl is perhaps best known for its figures of birds taken from the work of John James Audubon and for its hand-painted dinnerware on a red clay body (redware), first made in 1942. To make this dinnerware, Stangl covered the top surface of the redware body with a white engobe coating. The pattern was then stenciled on and subsequently carved into the surface. After a firing, the design was hand colored, covered with a clear glaze, and fired again. Most Stangl dinnerware pieces are marked with the Stangl name and the name of the pattern. Stangl dinnerware patterns of interest to collectors include:

"Amber Glo"

Designed by Kay Hackett, this unusual pattern features wavy lines that enclose stick figure trees with dots and commalike

Mark commonly found on Stangl dinnerware.

dashes. A 10-inch dinner plate should be priced between $22 and $26, and a cup and saucer is between $15 and $18. Hard-to-find pieces include:

6-cup coffee pot	*$75–$85*
Open skillet	*$45–$55*
14-inch round chop plate	*$75–$85*
Individual casserole	*$40–$50*

"Blueberry"

This pattern was designed by Kay Hackett and features a cluster of blueberries and leaves in the center of flatware items with a wide yellow rim around the outside edge. Factory-made seconds are available in this line, and they can be identified by their decoration, which is in shades of blue with no other colors used. Prices for these seconds are up to 50 percent less than the first quality examples. A 10-inch first quality dinner plate is $50 to $65, and a cup and saucer is $20 to $25. Hard-to-find items include:

14-inch round chop plate	*$100–$120*
1½-quart covered casserole	*$135–$165*
Coffeepot and lid	*$110–$130*
Open skillet	*$50–$65*

"Chicory"

Blue flowers with long brown stems decorate this grouping, which was designed by Kay Hackett. A 10-inch dinner plate should be valued at $40 to $50, and a cup and saucer $18 to $24. Hard-to-find items include:

10-inch oval divided vegetable bowl	*$75–$90*
Gravy boat and underliner	*$75–$90*
12½-inch round chop plate	*$65–$85*
Open skillet	*$40–$50*

Stangl 10-inch "Provincial" plate, $20 to $25. Photo courtesy of Kingston Pike Antique Mall, Knoxville, Tennessee.

"Country Garden"

Designed by Kay Hackett, this pattern featured a cluster of colorful flowers in the center of each plate. These flowers were depictions of yellow jonquils, bluebells, and buttercups. "Country Garden" was made with both the typical red (some call it brown) body and with a white body. The white body is rarer, and pieces are about 25 to 40 percent more valuable than the prices listed below. A 10-inch dinner plate should be valued between $25 and $35, and a coffee cup and saucer $15 to $20. Hard-to-find pieces include:

1¼-quart casserole, covered	$145–$165
13¾-inch platter	$90–$110
Coffeepot	$100–$125

"Country Life"

This is a charming pattern designed by Kurt Weise (adapted by Kay Hackett) featuring depictions of farm animals and farm life. One 10-inch dinner plate, for example, depicts a farmer's wife harvesting carrots, while another features a rooster. In addition, there were images of chickens, a farmhouse, a barn, a pig at a fence, a pony, and mallard ducks, among others. One of the more interesting pieces is the 14½-inch chop plate that features the depiction of a barn. Customers could have this piece customized with the name of their farms added to the design. This chop plate without the name is worth between $400 and $500—with the name, add another $100 or a bit more. The 10-inch dinner plate with the farmer's wife harvesting carrots is valued at between $200 and $275, while the 10-inch dinner plate with the rooster decoration is somewhat less at $125 to $150. A cup and saucer—the cup is decorated with a hen while the saucer has three eggs—is worth between $75 and $100. Hard-to-find pieces include:

8-inch coupe-shaped soup bowl, mallard	*$125–$150*
8-inch coupe-shaped soup bowl, mallard with another mallard diving for food with only the tail feathers above the water	*$250–$300*
12½-inch chop plate	*$450–$550*

"Fruit"

This pattern was designed by Kay Hackett and originated around 1945. The decoration consists of a composition of various colorful fruits including plums, cherries, apples, grapes, peaches, and pears. The original production had a yellow border with a brown edge, but later examples do not have this brown accent. This pattern is relatively plentiful, and a 10-inch diameter dinner plate should be valued in the $25 to $35 range, and a cup and saucer with a leaf decoration is worth $20 to $25. A cup and saucer with the image of a peach is worth a few dollars more. Hard-to-find items include:

8-inch lidded vegetable bowl	*$150–$200*
8-cup coffeepot	*$125–$150*

"Garden Flower"

As so many other Stangl patterns were, this one was designed by Kay Hackett. It has a yellow band around the outside rim on flatware with a dark green band around the verge. In the center there is a blooming flower, and individual shapes can be identified by the flower that was used to decorate them. The 10-inch dinner plate, for example, has a rose, as does the cigarette box, the coaster, the creamer, and the cup. The saucer just has leaves with no flower. Other flowers used were Balloon Flower (blue), Bleeding Hearts (pink), Campanula (purple), Calendula (yellow), Flax (blue), Morning Glory (blue), Phlox (pink), Sunflower (yellow), and Tiger Lily (yellow). A 10-

inch dinner plate is $35 to $45, and a cup and saucer is $18 to $22. Hard-to-find pieces include:

8³/₄-inch round vegetable bowl	$50–$60
5-cup teapot	$100–$120
11-inch round chop plate	$70–$85

"Magnolia"

This popular and commonly seen pattern has rust and white flowers with green leaves on a gray-green background. It was designed by Kay Hackett, and a 10-inch dinner plate is valued at $22 to $28, and a cup and saucer between $16 and $20. Hard-to-find items include:

14-inch chop plate	$65–$75
5-cup teapot	$90–$110
10-inch salad serving bowl	$45–$60

"Ranger" or "Cowboy and Cactus"

Also known as Stangl pattern number 3304, this distinctive pattern is thought to have been created by Tony Sarg. The larger pieces feature the full frontal silhouette of a bowlegged cowboy with the suggestion of six-guns on his hips. He is wearing an exaggerated ten-gallon hat and has a cactus to either side and hills behind. Smaller pieces such as the cup and saucer only have cactus and the hills, and the candleholders and regular salt and pepper shakers have only the "Ranger" colors and no other design. Colors are blue, brown, and yellow. This is an extremly hard-to-find pattern. A 10-inch dinner plate is worth $150 to $200, and a cup and saucer is $50 to $65. Harder-to-find pieces include:

Figural shaker, each	*$450–$600*
10-inch salad bowl	*$175–$225*
14-inch chop plate	*$200–$250*
Teapot	*$175–$225*

"Thistle"

Pink thistle flowers with leaves in two shades of green decorate this Kay Hackett design. It should be noted that the Japanese imitated this pattern using a decal instead of hand painting, and there is no carving on the look-alike. These are easy to identify because the ersatz items are marked "Japan." A 10-inch Stangl "Thistle" pattern dinner plate is $22 to $26, while a cup and saucer is $14 to $18. Hard-to-find items include:

Individual casserole	*$35–$45*
12-inch salad serving bowl	*$75–$85*
¼-pound butter dish	*$60–$75*
6-cup coffeepot	*$100–$120*

"Town and Country" or "Caughley"

This unusual dinnerware pattern was supposed to have the spattered look of metal enamelware from the 19th century. This pattern, which was made well into the 1970s, had a single solid color splattered on over a white engobe background. Colors found are blue, black, brown, green, yellow, crimson, and honey. Honey was added in 1977 and is probably the least desirable color. A 10-inch dinner plate is valued in the $40 to $50 range, and a cup and saucer at $25 to $35. Harder-to-find pieces include:

Tureen (originally sold as a four-piece set—tureen, lid, ladle, and chop plate to be used as the underplate)	*$575–$650*
15-inch platter	*$150–$175*
Coffeepot	*$100–$125*
Chop plate	*$90–$110*

Taylor, Smith and Taylor

Once again, there is some disagreement about the early history of this pottery company, which was located in Chester, West Virginia, with offices across the Ohio River in East Liverpool, Ohio. Some sources maintain that William Smith, Charles Smith, John Taylor, W. L. Taylor, Homer Taylor, and Joseph Lee founded this enterprise in 1899 as Taylor, Lee, and Smith. Shortly thereafter, the Taylors bought out Joseph Lee, and the company became Taylor, Smith and Taylor. Sometime between 1903 and 1906 (depending on the source consulted) the Smiths bought out the Taylors.

The Smiths ran the company until 1972, when it was sold to Anchor Hocking, which is known primarily as a maker of glassware. Anchor Hocking operated Taylor, Smith and Taylor until the company closed in 1981. Taylor, Smith and Taylor specialized in making dinnerware, kitchenware, and toilet wares from semiporcelain. Some Taylor, Smith and Taylor pieces are dated, but this practice was discontinued in the 1950s. Under the various company marks, there is often a grouping of three numbers, such as "9 44 3." The first two sets of numbers are a date, and in the example cited, the piece would have been made in September 1944. The last number represents the work team that made the piece.

Some of Taylor, Smith and Taylor's most sought-after lines of dinnerware include:

"Castle"

Made on Taylor, Smith and Taylor's "Garland" shapes, this underglaze decal decoration can be found in black, green, blue, and pink against an "Old Ivory" background. This design features a ruined English manor or "Castle," and the "Garland" pottery body has a rim embossed with leaves that spill over into the well slightly. It was made from around 1933 to 1942, and a 10-inch diameter plate is worth $18 to $22, and a cup and saucer is $16 to $20. Hard-to-find pieces include:

9½-inch oval vegetable bowl	$40–$50
9-inch round vegetable bowl	$45–$55
Teapot	$50–$65

"Lu-Ray Pastels"

Named for Virginia's famous Luray Caverns, this line of dinnerware originated in 1938 and was produced on two Taylor, Smith and Taylor shapes—"Empire" (a simple round shape with budlike finials on lidded pieces) and "Laurel" (a thin-edge shape). Originally, "Lu-Ray Pastels" came in Windsor blue, Persian cream (yellow), surf green, and Sharon pink. Chatham gray was added in 1948 and is considered to be the hardest-to-find color. While most pieces are solid color, decal decoration can be found on some pieces marked "Lu-Ray Pastels." A 10-inch diameter dinner plate in colors other than Chatham gray is valued in the $25 to $45 range, and a coffee cup and saucer is between $15 and $25. In Chatham gray a dinner plate is $75 to $85, a salad plate is $45 to $55, and a cup and saucer is $45 to $65. Hard-to-find pieces include (all prices listed below are for colors other than Chatham gray):

One of the most commonly found marks on Taylor, Smith and Taylor's "Lu-Ray Pastels."

Juice pitcher	$225–$275
10¼-inch diameter mixing bowl	$175–$225
1¼-quart covered casserole	$125–$180
10-inch compartmented grill plate	$40–$50
6¼-inch bowl	$350–$425
Handled cake plate	$100–$150
4-cup teapot	$220–$300
Demitasse cup and saucer	$65–$80
Cream soup and saucer	$125–$150
Flower arranger or epergne	$350–$425

NOTE: Some pieces marked "Coral-Craft" are actually pink "Lu-Ray" with simple white decorations in patterns called "Maple Leaf," "Tulip," "Floral Border," "Laurel Wreath," and "Chinese Temple." Prices for these "Coral-Craft" pieces are comparable to those of regular "Lu-Ray Pastels."

"Pebbleford"

Designed by John Giles, "Pebbleford" is a very distinctive dinnerware that has a solid color background with a sandlike fleck that gives the surface a speckled effect. Usually, the specks are brown. Most of the "Pebbleford" pieces are a rather plain coupe shape, but there is an interesting square cheese dish with a triangular lid. "Pebbleford" is a 1950s pattern, and the speckled glaze influenced dinnerware made by other companies. Colors include honey beige, mint green, pink, sand, teal, turquoise, sunburst yellow, granite, celery green, burnt orange, and marble white. "Pebbleford" pieces are usually marked "Pebbleford by Giles" with "Taylor, Smith and Taylor" above and "oven proof" below. A "Pebbleford" 10-inch diameter dinner plate should be valued at between $13 and $18, and a cup and saucer between $14 and $20. Hard-to-find pieces include:

1³/₄-quart round covered casserole	$75–$110
11-inch oval platter	$30–$45
Sauce boat with lid	$50–$60
Coffeepot	$55–$75
Cheese dish	$60–$100

"Silhouette"

This decal decoration of two men in colonial dress sitting across a tavern table from one another is the exact same decal used by Hall on its "Taverne" pieces that was discussed earlier. Both companies made this dinnerware as premiums for Hellick's Coffee, and occasionally a Taylor, Smith and Taylor "Silhouette" cup will turn up with "You are Drinking Hellick's Triple City Blend" on the back and a "Silhouette" decal on the front. The pieces made by Hall with this design are a little rarer than the Taylor, Smith and Taylor variety. A 10-inch T. S. & T. "Silhouette" 9¼-inch dinner plate is $30 to $40, while a flat cup and saucer is $22 to $30 and a footed cup and saucer is $24 to $32. Hard-to-find items include:

Covered butter dish, round	$70–$85
9-inch round vegetable bowl	$75–$100
12-inch oval platter	$50–$65

"Vistosa"

Created in 1938, but in production for only a few years, "Vistosa" is a solid color dinnerware that is thought to be Taylor, Smith and Taylor's attempt to get a share of Homer Laughlin's "Fiesta" market. The colors of mango red, cobalt blue, light green, and deep yellow are very similar to the hues found on "Fiesta." Ivory "Vistosa" items and examples with various decal decorations have been found as well. The shapes for "Vistosa" are very distinctive, with the flatware pieces having crimped piecrust-style edges, and many of the hollowware pieces have a similar treatment around their rims. "Vistosa" items are often marked with the name inside a circular device with a piecrust edge. A 10-inch diameter dinner plate in "Vistosa" should be valued in the $15 to $20 range, and a regular cup and saucer is about the same. Hard-to-find items include:

Gravy boat	*$150–$200*
8½-inch round vegetable bowl	*$100–$125*
12-inch diameter footed salad bowl	*$150–$200*

Vernon Potteries Ltd./Vernon Kilns

The Poxon China Company was founded in Vernon, California, in 1912 by George Poxon, who owned the ranch

SALAMINA
Designed by
Rockwell Kent
VERNON KILNS
Made in U.S.A.

One of the marks used by Vernon Kilns.

on which the pottery was built. At first, the company specialized in making tiles to be used on bathroom floors, but they also made some art pottery. At the beginning of World War I, the company switched to making dinnerware largely for commercial use in hotels and restaurants.

In 1931, Faye Bennison bought the pottery from Poxon and renamed the company Vernon Kilns. These were the years of the Great Depression, and times were tough for the company. The situation got worse in 1933, when an earthquake damaged the company's kilns and destroyed much of their stock on hand.

This disaster prompted a redesign of Vernon Kilns' products, and in the mid- to late 1930s, the company made a move into the area of producing art wares, which also influenced their dinnerware production. The company hired a number of designers, including Gale Turnbill, Don Blanding, and the important American illustrator and artist Rockwell Kent. Dinnerware inspired by Walt Disney's *Fantasia* was made as well and is among the most desirable of all the Vernon Kilns wares.

Blanding's designs are very recognizable because they often feature Hawaiian themes, with two having images of tropical flowers and two others emblazoned with pictures of colorful fish. Rockwell Kent designed for Vernon Kilns between 1938 and 1940, and during this period he was responsible for three dinnerware patterns that are highly sought after by modern collectors—"Salamina," "Moby Dick," and "Our America."

Faye Bennison sold Vernon Kilns to Metlox in 1958, and they later instituted a Vernonware Division to compete with their original "Poppytrail" dinnerware line. Some of the dinnerware patterns made by Vernon Kilns that are most desired by collectors include:

"Brown-Eyed Susan"

This charming pattern with its cheerful painting of brown-eyed Susans in yellow and brown was probably

Vernon Kilns "Brown-Eyed Susan" 12³/₄-inch diameter platter. The value is $40 to $50.

first introduced around 1940. A very few pieces can be found in the "Ultra" shapes, but most of the "Brown-Eyed Susan" pieces were made using the simpler "Montecito" forms. Perhaps the rarest items in this grouping are the candlesticks, which came in two varieties. One was made from a brass-mounted saucer, and the other was made from a brass-mounted cup. Both are so difficult to find that accurate pricing is impossible. A 10¹/₂-inch diameter plate in "Brown-Eyed Susan" is $25 to $30, and a cup and saucer is $14 to $20. Hard-to-find pieces include:

11-inch oval vegetable	*$50–$65*
Three-tier serving tray	*$55–$75*
Carafe with lid	*$40–$50*
Pepper mill	*$100–$125*

"Chatelaine"

This is a very unusual grouping of dinnerware designed by Sharon Merrill and first marketed in 1953. This pattern did not sell well because it was very out of the ordinary and was thought to be impractical. The shapes of the flatware in this line are squares and rectangles with a cluster of raised leaves placed at one or more corners. It came in four colors—bronze (a sort of rich chocolate brown), topaz (warm beige), jade (soft green with lighter green and beige accents on the leaves), and platinum (ivory with yellow and reddish brown accents on the leaves). Because it did not sell well, "Chatelaine" is a difficult pattern to find. Jade and platinum pieces are at the top of the price scales listed below, while bronze and topaz are at the bottom. The 10½-inch dinner plate came with either two or four corners decorated with the raised leaves. The examples with the leaves in just two corners are $25 to $35, while the ones with the leaves in four corners are $35 to $50. The coffee cup and saucer (flat base) is $28 to $40. Hard-to-find items include:

Teapot	*$250–$350*
14-inch chop plate	*$65–$95*
16-inch platter	*$85–$110*

"Early California" and "Modern California"

These are the line names of two solid color lines made by Vernon Kilns starting about 1937 and continuing until about 1950 or so. Both patterns were on the "Montecito" shape. "Early California" was made with bright colors in shades of yellow, turquoise, green, brown, dark blue, light blue, orange, and pink. Peach was added in 1946, and there was also ivory and maroon. Current collectors prefer pieces in orange, dark blue, brown, and maroon. In contrast, "Modern California" was basically the same ware with satin finish pastel colors in shades of azure, pistachio, yellow, orchid (lavender, some say light pink), gray ("Mist"), and beige. A 10½-inch diameter dinner plate in "Early/Modern California" is valued in the $15 to $30 range and a cup and saucer is $18 to $22. Hard-to-find pieces include:

6-cup teapot	*$70–$85*
13½-by-10½-inch grill plate	*$45–$60*
Sauce boat with lid	*$60–$75*
Tumbler	*$25–$40*
14-inch oval platter	*$60–$75*

"Fantasia"

Reportedly made in 1940 and 1941, the Disney "Fantasia" pattern is probably the rarest of all the Vernon Kilns dinnerware designs. There were several different patterns in this grouping, some of which featured winged fairies cavorting among flowers. "Ultra" shapes were

used except for the shaker, sugar bowl, and lidded creamer, which are on "Montecito." Colors are basically blue, maroon, or brown with hand-tinted detailing. Some of these pieces had only border designs with white centers, while other items were completely covered with decoration. "Fantasia" was made in a very limited number of shapes, and because of its rarity, assembling a complete set is considered to be a very difficult endeavor. The price for a 10½-inch dinner plate is $175 to $225, with a cup and saucer bringing about the same. Harder-to-find pieces include:

17-inch diameter chop plate	*$750–$900*
Muffin cover	*$800–$1,000*

Vernon Kilns "Early California" orange oval platter, $60 to $75. Item courtesy of Elaine Tomber Tindell.

"Frontier Days/Winchester '73"

Based on the "Montecito" shapes, this dinnerware grouping was inspired by the 1950 feature film *Winchester '73*, starring James Stewart and Shelley Winters. This pattern supposedly had "he-man" appeal, and each item had a transfer-printed western scene with the color applied by hand. The earlier pieces can be found with either a soft green or an ivory background, while the later items all have a green background. The designs were created by Paul Davidson and include images such as a cowboy on a fence, a prospector and his burro, a wagon train, a bank robbery, a buffalo hunt, a chuckwagon and camp-fire, cowboys roping and branding calves, a Native American on horseback, and a cowboy card game, among others. The name of this pattern was changed from "Winchester '73" to "Frontier Days" in 1953 due to a disagreement with the Winchester Arms Company over the use of their name. "Frontier Days/Winchester '73" is one of the most sought-after—and hard-to-find—of the Vernon Kilns patterns. Prices are generally three to four times higher than either "Early California" or "Modern California," and a 10½-inch diameter dinner plate should be valued in the $60 to $75 range, while a cup and saucer is just a bit more at $65 to $85. Hard-to-find items include:

Colossal 4-quart cup and saucer	$500–$600
13-inch diameter salad bowl	$175–$225
8½-inch diameter rimmed soup bowl	$100–$125
11-inch oval divided vegetable dish	$200–$225
Sandwich serving plate with central handle	$150–$175

"Fruitdale," "May Flower," and "Monterey"

All of these patterns are on Vernon Kilns' "Melinda" shape, which was designed by Royal Hickman and first produced in 1942. This shape is distinguished by the rope of embossed leaves around the outer edge of the flatware and the bases of the hollowware pieces. Pieces with handles have embossed leaves on the top of the handle, and the finials on lids are shaped to resemble flowers. "Monterey" is the "Melinda" shape with the embossing leaf shapes colored with red and blue. "Fruitdale" is the "Melinda" shape with the embossing left unaccented but with a large, exuberant grouping of fruit and flowers in the center of the flatware that takes up the entire well, and "May Flower" is much the same except the image contains only flowers. Prices for these patterns are comparable, but pieces of "Monterey" tend to be a little cheaper by a few dollars than the other two. A 10½-inch dinner plate should be valued at between $20 and $24, but a 9½-inch luncheon plate is a bit more at $24 to $28. A cup and saucer is $17 to $21. Hard-to-find items include:

14-inch chop plate	$42–$55
4-part leaf-shaped relish	$50–$75

Jam jar	*$60–$80*
Teapot	*$120–$160*

"Hawaiian Flowers/Lei Lani"

These are two of the four names given to a popular Don Blanding design that consists of a lotus blossom floral motif on two different Vernon Kilns shapes. "Hawaiian Flowers" is a design found in different colors of pink, blue, maroon, or mustard on Vernon Kilns' Ultra shape dinnerware. "Honolulu" is the same print but with hand-tinted yellow flowers on a blue background. "Hilo" is once again the same print, only this time it is in brown with hand-tinted flowers. "Lei Lani" has a maroon background with hand-tinted flowers and like the others is on the Ultra shape, which is often distinguished by its distinctive upside-down handles. "Hawaii," on the other hand, is the same as "Lei Lani" only it was placed on the company's Melinda shapes. Confusing? Yes, a bit. However, pieces are signed with "Aloha Don Blanding," the name of the company, and the particular pattern name, and this helps a great deal. These designs first appeared in 1939 and are mainly products of the 1940s. It should be noted that in 1947, the "Lei Lani" pattern was moved from the Ultra shapes to the newer "San Marino" shapes. There are many, many variables involved here, but in general a 10½-inch dinner plate in these patterns should be valued at $30 to $50, and a regular cup and saucer around $25 to $35. Hard-to-find items include:

7-inch sauce tureen or "tureenette"	*$150–$200*
¼-pound butter dish	*$85–$110*
Demitasse cup and saucer	*$60–$75*
5¾-inch rimmed fruit or dessert bowl	*$60–$75*
6-cup coffeepot	*$125–$175*

"Heavenly Days," "Tickled Pink"

Distinguished by small squares and crosses, "Heavenly Days" and "Tickled Pink" are the same pattern but in different color schemes. First made in 1955, "Heavenly Days" is done in aqua, pink, and mocha-charcoal with solid turquoise cups and serving pieces (casseroles have patterned lids), and "Tickled Pink" is in pink and charcoal with solid pink cups and serving pieces (again, the casseroles have patterned lids). Lids on the coffeepot and sugar bowl are respectively turquoise and pink. In the past, "Tickled Pink" has been a little more valuable than "Heavenly Days," but in recent years, that trend has reversed—but the difference is only a dollar or two here and there. A 10-inch diameter dinner plate is $15 to $20, and a cup and saucer is $12 to $16. Hard-to-find pieces include:

64-ounce pitcher	*$65–$75*
Round covered vegetable	*$70–$85*
14-ounce tumbler	*$35–$45*

"Moby Dick"

This may seem like a strange name for a dinnerware service, but the designs were taken from Rockwell Kent's illustrations for Herman Melville's novel *Moby Dick*. Interestingly, it became the most popular of Kent's three designs for Vernon Kilns. It is found on "Ultra" shapes and was decorated with largely monochromatic designs in shades of dark blue, orange, maroon, and brown. Blue and maroon are most commonly found, and orange is considered to be rare. The scenes are very stirring and feature such images as fully rigged sailing vessels, leaping porpoises, and soaring seabirds. This design was first made in 1938, and collectors are most interested in the large plates, which make a very impressive display in a cupboard or on a wall. Prices for "Moby Dick" are just a bit higher than for the Blanding "Hawaiian Flowers/Lei Lani" grouping. A 10½-inch diameter dinner plate is valued at $75 to $110, a luncheon plate at $70 to $85, and a cup and saucer at $40 to $65. Hard-to-find items include:

7-inch sauce tureen or "tureenette"	*$200–$250*
¼-pound butter dish	*$100–$125*
12-inch diameter chop plate	*$200–$250*

"Organdie"

One of Vernon Kilns' best sellers, "Organdie" (sometimes spelled "Organdy" by the company in its ads) is really a large grouping of patterns that collectors tend to lump under the descriptive designation "Plaid." "Organdie" originated in the late 1930s, and the original patterns were designed by Gale Turbull, whose signature appears on the back of each piece as part of the Vernon

Kilns mark. Each piece was hand painted under the glaze, and what follows is a list of the various "Plaid" Vernon Kilns patterns with their color scheme and style number when known.

1. "Coronation Organdie" (T-508), gray and rose
2. "Organdie," brown and yellow
3. "Organdie" (T-511), brown and yellow, but with more detailed painting than regular "Organdie"
4. "Organdie" (T-512), deep rose and green
5. "Organdie" (T-513), yellow and green
6. "Calico," pink and blue
7. "Gingham," green and yellow with a green border
8. "Homespun," green, rust, and yellow with a rust-colored border
9. "Tam O'Shanter," rust, chartreuse, and green with a green-colored border
10. "Tweed," gray and forest green
11. "Plaid" (T-515), gray and forest green
12. "Plaid" (T-604), rust brown and medium blue with a medium blue border

Of these "Organdie/Plaid" patterns, "Calico" and "Homespun" are the most valuable and prices are about 25 percent higher than for the other patterns in this grouping. An "Organdie" dinner plate is worth between $20 and $25, and a cup and saucer is $15 to $20. Hard-to-find items include:

Mug	$40–$50
5-cup teapot	$80–$100
Two-tier serving tray	$75–$95
10½-inch diameter salad bowl	$90–$110
Jumbo cup	$175–$200

"Our America"

This is a very ambitious Rockwell Kent series that divided the United States into eight regions—New England, Middle Atlantic, Southern Colonial, Mississippi River, Great Lakes, Plains and Mountains, Gulf, and Pacific—

and featured characteristic scenes from each region. There were more than 30 different designs on a cream background in four different colors—brown, dark blue, maroon, and green. Brown is the most commonly found color; green is the rarest. The most important and interesting piece in this grouping is considered to be the 17¼-inch chop plate, which shows the American eagle with outstretched wings above a shield. On the left is farmland, on the right is an urban landscape, and below is a map of the United States. This series is on "Ultra" shapes and came out in 1940. Prices are generally comparable to those for "Moby Dick."

"Salamina"

An unusual pattern taken from Rockwell Kent's book by the same name. It first appeared on the market in 1939. There was actually a real-life "Salamina." She was Kent's housekeeper when he lived in Greenland, and the book was Kent's chronicle of his life on that frozen island. Kent thought of Salamina as being a woman of great nobility and beauty who represented the better qualities of the women of Greenland. She is depicted in a very Art Moderne manner among glaciers and the northern lights, and the most famous image has a bird flying above one shoulder. Vernon Kilns' sales brochure proclaimed that "Salamina" was "Beautiful enough for the wall of an art museum." Pieces are hand tinted on "Ultra" shapes, and this pattern is considered to be one of the two most valuable Vernon Kilns designs. A 10½-inch dinner plate should be valued in the $150 to $175 range, and a cup and saucer at about the same price. Hard-to-find items include:

7-inch sauce tureen or "tureenette"	$600–$750
6-cup teapot	$450–$600
2-cup after-dinner size coffeepot	$550–$700
Jumbo cup and saucer	$300–$350

3

OTHER MAKERS OF AMERICAN EVERYDAY DINNERWARE

The "top ten" manufacturers list detailed in the preceding chapter is very subjective. For the collector who is interested in the products of another company, that company and its products are at the top of the only list that really matters.

There is no question that the companies that follow are important manufacturers and made dinnerware that is significant to a large number of enthusiasts. These potteries are treated more briefly than the companies in chapter 2, but they and their products are nonetheless essential to the overall story of American everyday dinnerware.

One of the marks used by the J. A. Bauer Pottery Company.

J. A. Bauer Pottery Company

In 1885, German immigrant John Andrew Bauer bought out an existing pottery in Paducah, Kentucky, and established his Paducah Pottery. This company specialized in making sanitary wares (e.g., chamber pots, etc.), whiskey jugs for the local distillers, bean pots, stoneware items, and flowerpots. Bauer was an asthma sufferer, and he spent his winters in California and became so enamored of the state that he moved there in 1909 and opened a pottery there in 1910.

Bauer made almost the same things in California that he was making in Kentucky, but his best sellers in the early days were flowerpots sold to growers as well as to home owners. Around 1912 or 1913, Bauer hired Danish immigrant Louis Ipsen to be a ceramics designer, and Ipsen began designing fancy flowerpots.

The glazes used on Bauer's flowerpots and other vessels were fairly basic and drab until the company hired ceramics engineer Victor Houser in 1929. Houser came up with some brightly colored glazes, which were tried on some rather sturdy dishes that Ipsen had been ordered to design. This marriage of Ipsen's dishes and Houser's bright glazes was analogous to the mating of the almost proverbial chocolate and peanut butter. Initially, Ipsen's dinnerware had been glazed with a transparent glaze over a yellow body, and the finished product is said to have looked like the under plates used to keep flowerpots from dripping on the floor. The addition of Houser's bright, flamboyant glazes took these dishes from ho-hum to glorious and from virtually unsellable to a hot new fad.

Before this time, dinnerware had been either too delicate or too expensive for casual indoor-outdoor use. The California lifestyle called for sturdy dinnerware that was colorful and appropriate for use either in a patio setting or in an informal dining room, and Bauer had invented the perfect product for this dual purpose. It originated in 1930 and was called "California Colored Pottery" or "Plain Ware."

"California Colored Pottery" was also perfect for the Depression Era during which it originated. It was cheerful and it was inexpensive, and Bauer saw it as something of a salvation during hard times, as did other pottery companies who were also struggling to survive the severe business downturn. "California Colored Pottery" was the basis for all the brands of sturdy solid color dinnerwares that were to follow.

In 1936 when Homer Laughlin introduced "Fiesta," the competition between the two companies was fierce. Bauer was well established in the western market, while Homer Laughlin was firmly entrenched in the East and Midwest. It was basically the old story of David against Goliath, with Bauer being David.

In 1928, Bauer purchased an old, two-story former winery building in Atlanta and refitted it to be a pottery. It was a bit of a makeshift effort, and in the beginning, the best that Bauer Atlanta could do was to snag a contract with the United States military to make clunky hotel-ware cereal bowls and tumblers for use by the troops in World War II. Today, one of these cereal bowls is worth about $30 to $40, and the 5½-inch-tall tumbler is about $5 more. The glory of Bauer's Atlanta operation was the art pottery they made, designed by Russel Wright. This was produced only in 1945 and 1946, and it is very hard to find. It should be mentioned that Mrs. Russel Wright— Mary Wright—wanted to get into the design business and created a dinnerware set for Bauer Atlanta to manufacture. It was called "Country Garden," and it never went into actual commercial production—but pieces do turn up from time to time. It was marked "Country Garden" (with the quotation marks) and below that was the signature "Mary Wright." Prices for "Country Garden" start at about $125 for a cup and saucer and go up from there. Bauer went out of business in 1962. They made a number of different dinnerware patterns, including "La Linda" (1939–1959) and "Monterey" (1936–1945), but "Ring" (1931 or 1932–early 1960s) is the one line that is most associated with this company and the one line that is most desired by today's collectors.

"Monterey Moderne"

Designed in the late 1940s by Tracy Irwin, this grouping was first produced by Bauer in 1949 and stayed in production until 1961. Unlike other Bauer solid color wares, "Monterey Moderne" had a distinctly modern design with coupe-shaped plates and a gloss glaze, and toward the end of the 1950s, some decal decorations were attempted. These are now rather rare and difficult to find. The most spectacular of these decals is the exuberant spray of Epiphyllum in pink, white, and green. On dinner plates, this decoration covers most of the center and has large opening blossoms among the suggestion of green leaves. The other decal design that is encountered is called "Barnyard" and features a red barn with a silo, a windmill, and a green field with a mailbox at the front edge. These pieces are hard to price because so few of them are found, but a 10½-inch dinner plate with the "Epiphyllum" design would be at least $50. Bauer did a lot of experimentation with "Monterey Moderne" glaze treatments, and two-tone examples can be found with one color on the top and another on the bottom. Other pieces may have a band of contrasting color used around a rim. Colors found on "Monterey Moderne" include yellow, pink, green, brown, chartreuse, burgundy, gray, and black. The most desired colors are burgundy and black or any of the two-tone pieces. A 10½-inch dinner plate should be valued at $30 to $40 in pink, and a cup and saucer in burgundy is $35 to $45. Hard-to-find items include:

10-ounce mug	*$45–$65*
13-inch diameter salad bowl	*$85–$110*
Round, covered butter dish	*$75–$100*
Three-tier serving tray	*$70–$90*
6-cup teapot	*$75–$100*

"Ring"

Introduced in 1931 (some sources say 1932), "Ring" was the company's most successful line of dinnerware, and it is said to be one of the main influences that led to the creation of "Fiesta" by the Homer Laughlin China Company some four or five years later. As the name suggests,

"Ring" is characterized by concentric rings that run around the edge of flatware pieces and up and down the sides of bowls and tumblers. "Ring" evolved from "California Colored Pottery," and it is thought that the rings were derived from the circular markings that occur when a piece of pottery is hand thrown on a potter's wheel. The original colors for "Ring" (pre–World War II) include light brown, Chinese yellow, orange red, jade green, cobalt blue, ivory, black, and white. Of these colors, the least desirable to collectors is probably the jade green (probably because it is the most available), and the most desirable are cobalt blue, black, and white—in that order. The "Ring" colors introduced after the end of World War II include red-brown, olive green, light blue, turquoise, chartreuse, gray, and burgundy. Two different shades of burgundy were made by Bauer—one was a dusty tone made before World War II, and the other was a purer tone made after the end of the war. Both shades of burgundy are highly desired, but gray is the least desired of the post-World War II hues. Reportedly, "Ring" was last made in the early 1960s. A "Ring" 10½-inch diameter dinner plate in burgundy is $120 to $145, while one in black would be $150 to $200. Cobalt blue and yellow dinner plates are a little less, with the blue examples being worth $100 to $120 and the yellow ones $95 to $110. A coffee cup and saucer is $50 to $100, but the after-dinner cup and saucer is rare and valued at three times that figure. Harder-to-find items include:

Barrel-shaped tumbler with metal handle, ivory	$200–$225
Cookie jar	$600–$750
5½-inch individual casserole	$150–$200
Beer jug	$450–$600
7-inch diameter mixing bowl	$150–$175

Crooksville China Company

The Crooksville China Company was organized in Crooksville, Ohio, in 1902 with 125 employees, and when they went out of business in 1959, there were 300. They specialized in making a very good grade of semiporcelain earthernware that at its best appears to be vitrified porcelain. Their finest, thinnest dinnerware products were marked "Stinthal China" with no obvious mention of the Crooksville name except for the initials "C. C. Co." that appears underneath the mark. Crooksville is known for its fine decal decoration, and there are at least two of these designs that attract current collectors' attention:

"Dairy Maid"

This is a charming decal decoration in the Pennsylvania Dutch manner. The design shows two figures standing up facing each other. The woman is churning butter, and the man is holding a cane under his arm. The two figures are surrounded by flowers, and behind the woman a bird perches on one of the blossoms. Below this is a heart, and the border is decorated with floral sprays. A 10-inch plate in this pattern is $18 to $22, and a cup and saucer is $24 to $28. Hard-to-find pieces include:

13³/₈-inch oval platter	$50–$65
9½-inch oval vegetable	$40–$55

"Petit Point House," "House," or "Cottage"

These are three names given to a charming decal design that appeared on many different Crooksville shapes. This

Crooksville China Company "Petit Point House" 11-inch diameter mixing bowl, $30 to $45. Item courtesy of Kingston Pike Antique Mall, Knoxville, Tennessee.

pattern features the image of a cottage and colorful garden that looks like it has been rendered in petit point stitchery. Pieces are accented with a red ring around the design, or in some cases, around both the design and the item's outer edge. "Petit Point House" is a pattern that was used mainly in the late 1930s and 1940s. A 9¾-inch diameter plate is valued at $20 to $25, and a standard cup and saucer at $25 to $30. Harder-to-find items include:

11-inch oval platter	$65–$75
Cookie jar	$75–$100
Round vegetable dish	$50–$65
Batter jug with lid	$100–$125
Pie serving plate	$70–$85

"Silhouette"

Similar to Hall's "Taverne" pattern, this design shows two figures seated in chairs at a table. There is a report that one of these figures is a female, but this is doubtful since both figures are showing too much leg in their colonial-style garb with absolutely no skirts in sight. In any event, the dog begging at the figure's feet is the distinctive part of this pattern that sets "Silhouette" apart from "Taverne." "Silhouette" was first made at Crooksville in the early 1930s and is usually found on pieces with a pale yellow background accented with a black line border around the edge or rim (the Hall pattern is on white with a black rim or edge). "Silhouette" can be found on several Crooksville shapes, and a 9½-to 10-inch diameter dinner plate retails for $15 to $20, and a regular cup and saucer for about the same. Harder-to-find pieces include:

Sandwich tray with chrome frame	$45–$60
Footed teapot	$65–$100
Coffeepot with china drip	$125–$150
Mug, tankard style	$50–$65
4- or 6-inch round casserole	$50–$65

Dedham Pottery

The Dedham Pottery of East Dedham, Massachusetts, was the successor to the famous Chelsea Pottery of Chelsea, Massachusetts. This firm was founded in 1866 by Alexander W. Robinson and managed by Hugh Robinson. The company moved to East Dedham in either 1895 or 1896, depending on the source consulted, and remained in business in that location until 1943. Originally, the company had made art pottery, but after moving to East Dedham, they became a two-kiln operation with one kiln making art pottery and the other making some of the most sought-after American everyday dinnerware.

Some may quibble that Dedham "Crackleware" was introduced too early to be included in a discussion of dinnerware from the 1920s and later, and still others may say that Dedham "Crackleware" is more art ware than everyday dinnerware. But despite these equivocations, "Crackleware" was produced into the 1940s and was never intended to be anything more than artistically made pottery designed for use on an informal table as everyday dinnerware. Collectors should be aware that modern reissues and reproductions do exist (see *www.specialofsudbury.com/dpottery* and *www.bestofnewengland.com* for Web sites featuring Dedham reproductions).

"Crackleware"

The Dedham dinnerware body was high-quality gray stoneware with an intentional crackle glaze in imitation of Chinese pottery, and the tiny fissures in this glaze were often accentuated by rubbing in lampblack. The decoration was done freehand and generally consisted of a border around the edge of the piece with designs painted in cobalt blue. There were a number of patterns with the most commonly seen being a border of rabbits parading around the edge. The rabbit is reportedly the design of Joseph Linden Smith, and it was so popular that the image was adopted as the company's trademark. It is said that the Robinsons wanted the rabbit to be drawn the same way every time to achieve continuity. To achieve this goal, they had the rabbit carved into the mold so that a raised rabbit design would be produced around the rim, and this would allow the decorators just to color in the outlines. Unfortunately, the pieces with the slightly raised rabbits on them did not release from the mold well so this practice was discontinued. It should also be mentioned that on early pieces the bunnies are facing left, but on later pieces they face right. Examples with left-facing rabbits are about 20 percent more valuable than later pieces with right-facing rabbits. Other border patterns on Dedham "Crackleware" include apple, lobster, crab, bird in potted orange tree, butterfly, butterfly with flower, cat, cherry, chick, duck, dolphin, magnolia, peacock, polar bear, snow tree, strawberry, swan, turkey, turtles, wild rose, water lily, and others plus variations on these themes. A 10-inch diameter dinner plate with the standard rabbit border should be valued in the $350 to $500 range, while one with a crab motif is $900 to $1,200. An 8½-inch luncheon plate with a chick design is $2,000 to $2,500, and one the same size with a dove is $1,500 to $2,000. A rabbit pattern cup and saucer is $250 to $325, and one with a polar bear is $500 to $750. Hard-to-find pieces include:

The famous rabbit mark found on much of Dedham's dinnerware.

18-inch platter with lobster design	*$2,500–$3,000*
Rice bowl, bird in potted orange tree	*$1,200–$1,400*
6-inch plate with peacock design	*$3,000–$3,500*
6-by-9-inch tureen, azalea	*$1,400–$1,600*
7½-inch child's plate, cat	*$4,000–$5,000*

One of the
marks used by
W. S. George.

W. S. George

W. S. George Pottery Company

The East Palestine Pottery Company was founded in East Palestine, Ohio, in 1880 but did not acquire this name until 1884. Primarily, they made yellowware and pieces with a Rockingham glaze (in the United States, "Rockingham" is a brown mottled glaze that may have streaks and splotches of other colors). For years, this company was on the brink of bankruptcy, but when George E. Sebring became the manager in 1893, the company's financial position took a turn for the better. Sebring left in 1896 and here is where the story becomes a little vague. William Shaw George may have leased the company in 1898, or he may have gone to work for the Sebring brothers as the manager of East Palestine. Whichever it was, George owned the East Palestine Company by either 1903 or 1904 and changed the name to the W. S. George Pottery Company.

After recovering from some health problems, George began an expansion program that added two pottery plants in Pennsylvania and another in East Palestine. W. S. George produced large quantities of hotel ware, toilet wares, and semiporcelain dinnerwares. Collectors are interested in several of the W. S. George decal designs including one called "Breakfast Nook" or "Springtime." Three shape lines known as "Bolero," "Georgette" or "Petal," and "Rainbow" came in either solid color or decal decorated, and these interest collectors as well. The W. S. George Pottery closed about 1960, with several sources saying it was in the late 1950s.

"Basketweave"

As the name indicates, this W. S. George shape is distinguished by a broad band in basket weave around the edge of flatware, the rim of pitchers and the body of other hollowware pieces. This design was introduced in 1930 and can be found in solid colors of blue, brown, green, maple bisque, and yellow. Decal decorations usually were applied to either the yellow or green colors. In 1938, "Pastels Plus" were introduced and these were "Basketweave" with colored rims and decal designs such as "Dallas" (bluebonnets arranged to make a five-pointed star), "Fresno" (a "Willow" pattern), "Lancaster" (ladies in 19th-century style fashions), "Omaha" (stylized wheat), and "Taos" (basket of flowers). A 9⅛-inch dinner plate is valued at $14 to $20, and a cup and saucer $12 to $18. Hard-to-find pieces include:

9⅜-inch oval vegetable	*$30–$40*
Casserole with lug handles	*$35–$45*

"Bolero"

Introduced in 1933, "Bolero" was distinguished by its elegant fluted shapes. The early shapes included an oval teapot, casserole, sugar, and creamer, but these were restyled in the late 1930s into round forms. The earlier oval forms are much more desired by collectors than the later round ones. One of the most distinctive "Bolero" pieces is an oyster shell–shaped relish dish. Several of these could be arranged in a pleasing fan design to make an attractive centerpiece. "Bolero" was decorated in a number of different decal designs, including "Flight" (flying geese), "Pals" (two fish), "Cherry Blossom," and "Garcia" (a Mexican-style pattern with flowers and pots on a serape). In 1934, "Bolero Faience" was introduced, which was a solid color version of this shape. Officially, it came in lemon yellow, alabaster, and turquoise, but pieces in cobalt blue and brown have been found. A 9¼-inch dinner plate in the "Bolero" shape is $15 to $25, and a cup and saucer is $12 to $20. Hard-to-find pieces include:

Oval teapot	*$70–$85*
Round teapot (restyled)	*$50–$70*
9-inch round vegetable bowl	*$30–$40*
Oval-covered onion soup bowl (doubles as individual casserole)	*$50–$75*

"Breakfast Nook" or "Springtime"

This charming design depicts a flower-bedecked fence in front of an open latticework window with a birdcage and flowerpot. On plates, this romantic scene is set off to one side near the edge and conjures up an image of a stage setting where a mid-20th-century Juliet will soon appear (probably looking something like Harriet Nelson of *Ozzie and Harriet* fame). This pattern is associated with W. S. George's scalloped "Lido" and "Rainbow" shapes and was introduced in the early 1930s. It can also be found on "Argosy" shaped dinnerware, which has both round and square (i.e., rounded corners) plates. This pattern was promoted by the Chicago department store Daniel Low & Company as "Springtime." A 10-inch dinner plate in this pattern is valued in the $18 to $30 range, while a standard cup and saucer retails in the range of $15 to $25. Hard-to-find pieces include:

Teapot	*$45–$60*
9½-inch casserole	*$30–$45*
Gravy boat	*$70–$85*
Covered round vegetable	*$125–$150*

"Elmhurst"

Introduced in 1936, this is a paneled shape with a slight scallop to the rim. It can be found in pastel solid colors, which were introduced in 1939 and feature apple green, blue, maple sugar, pink, turquoise, and yellow. Decal decorations found on this shape include "Harvest" (stylized wheat), "Tasket" (a basket of flowers), and "Wing" (birds perched on a flower trellis). A 10-inch dinner plate is valued at $20 to $25, and a cup and saucer is $15 to $20. Hard-to-find items include:

9-inch round vegetable bowl	*$40–$50*
Teapot	*$50–$60*

"Georgette" or "Petal"

First made in 1933, this shape has flat panels around the flatware pieces that look like petals surrounding a flower's center—thus the popular name "Petal." Initially, this shape was decorated with a wide range of decals, including "Federal" (stars and an eagle), "Jolly Roger" (ships depicted in black silhouette), and "Peasant" (woman in a polka-dotted apron and a man in a field). The solid color line originated in 1947 and came in shades of aqua, dark green, chartreuse, gray, light green, maroon, medium blue, pink, and yellow. A 10-inch diameter dinner plate is $15 to $20, while a regular cup and saucer is $15 to $25. Hard-to-find pieces include:

Jumbo cup and saucer	$40–$50
Casserole	$35–$45
Sugar bowl	$35–$45
9-inch oval vegetable bowl	$35–$50
9-inch round vegetable bowl	$45–$60

"Rainbow"

Introduced in 1934, this line was decorated with a number of different decals, such as "Iceland Poppy," "Reflection" (a weeping willow and its reflection), "Hollyhock" (six groups of blossoms in shades of orchid, blue, and yellow), and "Fantasy" (blue bowls filled with an arrangement of poppies). There was a special solid color line called "Rainbow Petitpoint" in which the decoration was embossed and had the look of needlework. These pieces came in cobalt blue, light green, yellow, and chocolate brown. Chocolate brown is the hardest "Rainbow Petitpoint" color to find. This was a line with very few pieces, and prices are very modest. A 9-inch diameter plate is $10 to $14, and a cup and saucer about the same. Regular solid color "Rainbow" came in blue, green, pink, tan, and yellow. Prices are just a bit higher than those of "Rainbow Petitpoint," and a 9-inch dinner plate (the 10-inch size was a platter, and no 10-inch dinner plate was made) should be valued between $14 and $20, and a cup and saucer a dollar or two less. Hard-to-find items include:

| Round gravy | $18–$25 |
| Pair of candleholders | $25–$35 |

Iroquois China Company

The Iroquois China Company was founded in Syracuse, New York, in 1905. The history of this company is rather sketchy until 1947, when they began manufacturing "Casual China," which was designed by Russel Wright (see Harker's "White Clover" line also). Prior to that, Iroquois had manufactured mainly commercial and hotel dinnerware. In addition, collectors are interested in the five dinnerware lines designed for Iroquois in the 1950s by Ben Seibel. These lines are "Impromptu," "Informal," "Inheritance," "Intaglio," and "Interplay." Of these lines, "Interplay" is the rarest, followed by "Inheritance" and "Intaglio." "Impromptu" and "Informal" are far easier to find. Iroquois ceased production in 1969.

"Carrara Modern"

Introduced in 1955, this modern-looking pattern with veins of color running through either a white or a dark gray is supposed to look a bit like the famous Carrara marble. It came in three color schemes—gray with white veining, white with gold veining, and white with black veining. Although the gray and white color scheme is very dramatic, the value of the white and black examples are a little higher than the other two combinations. Shapes are very simple in this pattern, and a 9½-inch dinner plate is valued at $18 to $22, while a cup and saucer is about the same. Hard-to-find pieces include:

Covered oval divided vegetable dish	$90–$120
Centerpiece	$70–$85
14-inch chop plate	$40–$60
Covered jug	$60–$75

"Casual China"

This is a huge line that went through three distinct periods of development. The first period is characterized by pieces that have a heavier body than later items and a very distinctly speckled, frothy-looking glaze. These pieces are found in four colors: oyster white, powder blue, brown, and chartreuse yellow. In 1949, the speckled glaze was abandoned, the body was thinned down considerably, and new colors were added. The colors introduced in 1949 were oyster gray, parsley green, avocado yellow, sugar white, nutmeg brown, and ice blue. In 1950, another color, ripe apricot, was added. All of this change in body and color caused a change in advertising strategy. The line was said to be extremely durable, and to reflect this concept, the name was changed for a time to "Duralaine Casual China." The idea was that the consumer could use this china for baking and storage as well as for serving,

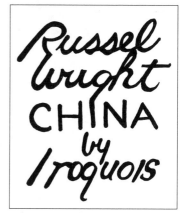

Russel Wright mark used on Iroquois China's "Casual China."

and if a piece was broken, the company offered to replace it. The third reinvention of "Casual China" began in the 1950s, with Wright tinkering with the designs and making some changes. One of the most noticeable of these changes was the disappearance of lids with pinch grips. These were replaced with knobs because customers were complaining that the pinch grips were hard to use. Colors introduced in the 1950s were charcoal, pink sherbet, lettuce green, and lemon. In the mid-1950s, floral-decorated dinnerware was very popular with American customers, and Iroquois pressured Wright to add some decal decorations of flowers. He did, and some pieces with decals were made in limited numbers, but as a general rule, these are not as popular with collectors as the pieces that have only the solid colored glazes. In the 1960s, three new colors were added to Iroquois "Casual"—brick red, aqua, and mustard gold. Often, cantaloupe is included in this group, but it was actually introduced in 1959. Of these shades, brick red and aqua are considered to be rare, while cantaloupe is thought of as being hard to find. Mustard gold is also uncommon, but it does not appeal to the majority of collectors in the same way that some other colors do. A 10-inch diameter dinner plate in charcoal is valued in the $25 to $30 range, while one in oyster white is approximately $5 more. In brick red and aqua, a 10-inch dinner plate is $80 to $95. An original cup and saucer in charcoal is worth between $15 and $20, but the after-dinner cup and saucer in charcoal is $500 to $600. In brick red and aqua, the re-

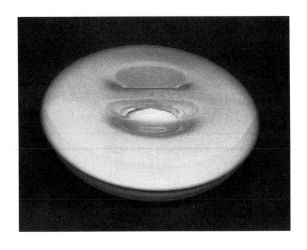

Iroquois China Company's "Casual China" divided casserole in ice blue, $35 to $45. Note the pinch grip on the lid. Item courtesy of Jane Roney.

designed cup and saucer are $80 to $95—just like the dinner plates in the same colors. Hard-to-find pieces include:

Pitcher, redesigned, brick red, aqua	$2,200–$2,750
Pitcher, redesigned, pink sherbet	$350–$400
Salt and pepper mill set, lettuce green	$500–$650
Salt and pepper mill set, ice blue	$500–$650
Mug, blue	$100–$120
Mug, lettuce green	$200–$220
Mug, white	$160–$175
4-cup teapot, cantaloupe	$1,000–$1,200
6-cup teapot, blue	$220–$250
Sandwich serving plate with central handle, cantaloupe	$60–$75
Dutch oven, white	$350–$375
½-pound covered butter, charcoal	$110–$125
½-pound covered butter, lettuce green	$200–$225

"Impromptu"

Designed by Ben Seibel with clean modern lines, "Impromptu" was introduced in 1956. It came decorated with a large number of different designs including "Blue Doves" (two doves facing each other among foliage), "Aztec" (triangles around the edge in shades of gold and orange), "Blue Vineyard" (flowers and berries around the rim in blue), "Georgetown" (floral band in green and brown), "Jardiniers" (1950s modern-looking stylized hanging baskets of flowers in gray, coral, and pink), "Luau" (tropical flowers in red with mustard accents), and "Harvest Time" (three autumn leaves—one orange, one gray, one yellow). "Impromptu" pieces are marked with the line name and the name of the designer plus "Iroquois." A 10-inch "Impromptu" dinner plate is $15 to $25, and a cup and saucer is about the same. Hard-to-find items include:

12-inch divided vegetable	*$65–$75*
Vinegar and oil set	*$70–$85*
Coffeepot	*$60–$80*
Covered vegetable	*$85–$100*

"Informal"

This Ben Seibel–designed line is duo-colored, with the outside of hollowware pieces, the inside of cups, and the underside of flatware items being covered with a solid color. In the case of a pattern like "Blue Diamonds," the design is large diamond shapes containing a stylized floral design done in blue and charcoal gray with a little yellow accent on a white background. The undecorated backs and sides in this pattern are in solid Bristol blue, and some pieces have no design but are all duo-tone Bristol blue and white. Another pattern found on "Informal" is "Lazy Daisy," which has a scattering of daisies with attached stems and leaves in blue, green, and yellow. The undecorated backs and sides in this pattern are in the same yellow used for the flowers. Some of the other patterns found on "Informal" are "Old Orchid" (scattering of fruit, grapes, and leaves in blue and brown with a brown reverse color), "Rosemary" (pink roses and green leaves with a gray-green reverse), and "Sleepy Hollow" (blue, gold, and green flowers with a citron yellow reverse). "Informal" pieces are marked with the line and designer name, and prices are comparable with "Impromptu."

NOTE: Two of the other Ben Seibel lines, "Inheritance" and "Intaglio," are also comparably priced with "Impromptu"; both are identifiable with the line name used as part of the Iroquois mark. Very little is known about the last Seibel line, "Interplay," and it is not possible to provide reliable prices.

Russel Wright
mark used on
Paden City
Pottery
Company's
"Highlight."

Paden City Pottery Company

Located in Paden City, West Virginia, the Paden City Pottery started operating in either 1907 or 1914, depending on the source consulted. The company was founded by George Lasell, and it is best known for its semi-porcelain dinner- and kitchenwares. This company is credited by many with being the first pottery maker to use a decal decoration under the glaze. This method of application helped protect the decal from later damage that might be incurred during household use. Unfortunately, application under the glaze limited the range of colors that could be used in the manufacturing process because most colors were destroyed in the intense firing process. The Paden City decals that were applied under the glaze are said to look like they were hand painted, and beginning collectors have been known to mistake these decals for genuine hand-done designs. It should also be noted that Paden City applied decal decorations over the glaze as well, which was the standard practice of the time. Collectors should be aware that there is a Paden City Glass Manufacturing Company, and those interested in glass call this company "Paden City" just as dinnerware enthusiasts call the pottery company by the same name—so don't be confused. The Paden City Pottery Company closed in 1963. Some lines of interest to current collectors are:

"Caliente"

This is yet another solid color dinnerware cast in the "El Patio," "Ring," and "Fiesta" image. "Caliente" was introduced in 1936, the same year as "Fiesta," and it was described in print ads as "Colorful Gay Caliente Ware" and as "Rainbow Caliente" (*caliente* is Spanish for "hot"). It was done initially on Paden's City's "Elite" shapes, but in 1938, most of this dinnerware design was put on the new "Shell-Krest" shape. "Caliente" can be found in tangerine red, turquoise green, sapphire blue, and lemon yellow. A 10½-inch dinner plate is valued in the $14 to $18 range, and a cup and saucer at just a few dollars less. Harder-to-find pieces include:

Teapot ("Shell-Crest" shape)	*$60–$75*
Covered casserole	*$40–$50*
14-inch platter	*$60–$75*

"Highlight"

Designed by Russel Wright, this pattern was made for a short time only between 1951 and 1953. It was manufactured in both a matte and a glossy finish in citron, pepper, nutmeg, blueberry, white, and green. The latter two colors were added late and are the two hardest-to-find shades. For some reason, "Highlight" seems to damage easily, and chips are found with some regularity. The Paden City Glass Manufacturing Company mentioned earlier made some glass pieces that were meant to coordinate with "Highlight." Called "Snow Glass," there was a saucer, three sizes of tumblers, a salad plate, a round vegetable bowl, a pitcher, a fruit dish, and lids for the pottery sugar bowl and vegetable bowl. These items are very hard to find, and a pitcher sells for around $2,000, while a vegetable bowl fetches $850. A "Highlight" dinner plate in both green and white is valued in the $45 to $60 range, in other colors, $25 to $35. A pepper-colored cup should be valued between $25 and $35, but with a white "Snow Glass" saucer another $100 needs to be added (a white pottery saucer adds $12 to $15). Harder-to-find items include:

Salt and pepper shakers	*$1,000–$1,500*
Covered vegetable bowl	*$150–$175*
Cover to vegetable bowl, "Snow Glass"	*$500–$600*
Pitcher, "Snow Glass"	*$1,600–$2,000*

NOTE: "Highlight" pottery pieces are marked with the "Russel Wright" signature, and sometimes with the name of the distributor "Justin Tharaud & Son." Sometimes, the Paden City name will appear as well.

"Shell-Krest" or "Shell-Crest"

This line is an outgrowth of Paden City's "Elite" shape, which has plain edges on the flatware but the hollowware items have shell-shaped handles, finials, and feet. In 1937, it was decided to develop flatware that had slight shell-like lug protrusions on either side and shell-like embossing around the edge. This line was named "Shell-Krest" or "Shell-Crest" and was manufactured in a variety of pastel colors such as azure, celedon, cream, and rose. After 1938, this shape was also used for the "Caliente" line, which is discussed above, and the two lines—one pastel, the other brightly colored—were designed to be complementary. "Shell-Krest" was also decorated with a number of decals, such as "Cornflower," "Cottage Shelf" (featuring shelves filled with knick-knacks), "Good Earth" (the image of a farmer plowing a field), "Spinning Wheel" (a woman sitting at a spinning wheel), "Nasturtium," "Rosetta" (a rose among other flowers), and "Village" (depicting houses and trees). Pieces of this line are generally marked with the name "Shell-Krest" or "Shell-Crest" contained within a shell that resembles a partially opened fan. Although the pastel-colored "Shell-Krest" is a little harder to find, the prices are comparable with those of "Caliente."

"Shenandoah"

This is one of the Paden City groupings that often has underglaze decals that are supposed to look like they are hand painted. Sometimes, however, overglaze decals were used on "Shenandoah." This line was first made in 1944, and pieces appear generally on the New Virginia flatware shapes. Most of the decal decorations are based on floral or botanical themes, such as "Cosmos," "Poppy," "Strawberry," "Morning Glory," "Jonquil," and "Minerva Rose." "Shenandoah" pieces are usually marked "Shenandoah Ware" either with that phrase by itself or above the Paden City circular mark that has the image of a roof with a big conical chimney and the words "underglaze" below. A 9-inch diameter dinner plate should be valued at $15 to $20, and a cup and saucer is about the same. Hard-to-find items include:

Chop plate	$40–$50
Teapot	$65–$85
9½-inch diameter lug-handled casserole	$45–$65

"Willow"

As has been said before, the "Willow" pattern was made by a number of companies primarily in the United States, England, and Japan. The typical version of this very popular pattern has a blue transfer print or decal of an Asian scene with willow trees, houses, a bridge, and birds on a white background, but Paden City put a new spin on this old design. This involved etching a photographic image of the typical "Willow" configuration into the surface of the plate and then covering the entire surface with a dark blue glaze so the pattern shows through as shallow indentions. Paden City's "Willow" is different from all the dinnerware mentioned previously in that it was made in only seven shapes—9-inch plate, 7-inch plate, cup, saucer, 10-inch platter, cereal bowl with lug handles, and 9-inch soup bowl. These were intended to make either a breakfast or a luncheon set, and they were sold in boxed sets with each set containing six each of all the items except one each of the salad bowl and platter. A 9-inch dinner (luncheon/breakfast) plate is $25 to $35, and a cup and saucer is $18 to $25. Hard-to-find items include:

10-inch platter	*$35–$50*
9-inch salad bowl	*$40–$60*

Pfaltzgraff

Located in York, Pennsylvania, Pfaltzgraff is reportedly the oldest continuously operating family-owned pottery in America. There is some debate about the actual year this company was founded, but 1811 is one of the most commonly quoted dates. However, some say the actual date should be 1805. Originally, the Pfaltzgraff family was from the Pfalz area of the Rhineland in Germany, and a representation of the family castle, which is still in existence, is seen as an outline of one of the company's marks. In the beginning, Pfaltzgraff made redware and stoneware for household use and storage purposes. The potteries (there were several working in various locations) served the communities that surrounded them, and there are charming stories of the Pfaltzgraffs allowing parties to be held in their buildings in the wintertime because the heat from the kilns kept the rooms warm and comfortable. In addition, it is said that they allowed people to slowly bake beans in their kilns while they were being heated to the high temperatures necessary to fire the stoneware. Pfaltzgraff adopted the name "Pfaltzgraff Pottery Company" in 1896, and as time passed and competition from foreign potteries increased, Pfaltzgraff's product line began to change. At one point, they special-

One of the marks used by Pfaltzgraff showing the outline of the family castle, which still exists in Germany.

ized in making animal feeders and redware flowerpots, but in the 1930s, kitchen and art wares (art pottery was made from 1931 to 1937) were added to the line, and dinnerware became a big part of their production starting in the 1950s. Some lines of interest to collectors are:

"Country-Time"

Advertised as "America's complete line of serving accessories . . . complete with place settings," this dinnerware grouping was designed by Ben Seibel and introduced in 1952. This is the same year the Roseville Pottery Company premiered Seibel's "Raymor" line, and the "Country-Time" cup with closed handles is the same as the one used for "Raymor." "Country-Time" was an extensive line with some unusual features, such as platters that could be hung from the wall and metal stands for accessory items that came in either copper, nickel, or brass plating. "Country-Time" was manufactured in solid colors of Aztec blue or teal blue but pieces can be found that were decorated with underglaze designs of either a starburst or a fruit and leaf motif. These designs were either done in blue with a saffron yellow or smoke gray glaze or in brown with a white glaze. A 10-inch dinner plate is worth $22 to $28 and a cup and saucer is $15 to $22. Hard-to-find items include:

Rectangular three-part casserole with three lids	$110–$125
6-quart tureen	$85–$110
2-quart casserole	$50–$65
28-cup coffee samovar	$100–$145

"Gourmet"

Pfaltzgraff's "Gourmet" line was first introduced as kitchenware in 1940, but in 1950 "Gourmet Royale" came out, which included dinnerware with a rich brown glaze made from Albany slip (originally made from a brown clay discovered in Albany, New York) with accents of a white drip. Now called just "Gourmet" or "Gourmet

Brown," this is a very extensive line that is becoming more popular with collectors. A 10-inch dinner plate is $20 to $25, and a cup and saucer is $10 to $15. Hard-to-find pieces include:

2-quart casserole, hen-on-nest style	*$85–$100*
3-quart bean pot with metal warmer stand	*$60–$75*
20-cup coffee samovar	*$100–$125*
Lazy Susan, four dishes, and 2-quart casserole, wooden base	*$85–$100*

"Yorktowne"

At last report, this pattern is still in production. It was designed by Maury Mountain and was introduced in 1967 and is based on Pfaltzgraff's early 19th-century blue decorated stoneware. Flatware items usually have a blue band around the edge of the well, and in the center there is a blue flower against a gray-blue matte glazed background. The early version of this flower was a Pennsylvania Dutch–style tulip, but later pieces have two blossoms arching out of several leaves (depending on the piece, there may be only one blossom or no blossom at all, just leaves). Prices for both the new and the old style are the same on the secondary market. A 10-inch plate is $8 to $12, and a cup and saucer is $5 to $7. Hard-to-find pieces include:

Tureen, ladle, and underplate	*$100–$125*
18-inch turkey platter	*$50–$65*
2½-quart bean pot	*$50–$65*

Purinton Pottery

In 1936, Bernard Purinton purchased the East Liverpool Potteries Company in Wellsville, Ohio, and founded Purinton Pottery. This facility proved inadequate for the company's needs, and a new plant was constructed in Shippenville, Pennsylvania, which became operational in 1941. This company did not use decal or transfer decoration on its dinnerware, but only used hand painting under the glaze. In the late 1950s, the company ran into trouble and there was an attempt to allow Taylor, Smith and Taylor to manage the plant, but Purinton closed in 1959. Like the pieces hand painted at Southern Potteries under the "Blue Ridge" trade name, the colorful painting on Purinton wares tend to have a very spontaneous and

naïve look that is very attractive to collectors. Some Purinton lines are so rare that it is impossible to provide accurate prices for them. One of these is "Palm Tree," which features palm trees with brown trunks and water in the background. A single 9¾-inch dinner plate in this pattern is at least $300 and may be somewhat higher. Another rare pattern is "Peasant Garden" (thick wavy lines of red alternate with laurel leaves to decorate the rim of the flatware, with red and yellow flowers in the well), and a dinner plate is at least $150. More readily available Purinton patterns include:

"Apple"

This is said to be Purinton's first and most successful pattern. The design consists of a large apple with a thick red band surrounding an ivory and brown center. This is accented with green leaves and brown twigs. Do not confuse this with Purinton's "Fruit" pattern, which also features an apple, but for this pattern, the apple is solid red with no ivory and brown center and the apple is usually depicted beside a yellow pear (pineapples and grapes also can appear). For most collectors, "Fruit" is a less desirable pattern than "Apple" and is less expensive. "Apple" was made in a large number of forms, and it is possible to find such things as canister sets, cruets, marmalade jars, cookie jars, and even a "tumble-up." A "tumble-up" is a water bottle with a tumbler that can be inverted over the neck of the bottle as a cover. It was designed to sit on a bedside table for a refreshing midnight thirst quenching. An "Apple" 9¾-inch dinner plate is $35 to $45, and a cup and saucer is $20 to $25. Hard-to-find items include:

11-inch oval salad serving bowl	$80–$95
Cookie jar, square, ceramic top 12¼	$250–$300

"Heather Plaid" and "Normandy Plaid"

"Heather Plaid" consists of two crisscrossing bands of turquoise accented with thinner lines of burgundy and yellow. "Normandy Plaid" is the same pattern with crisscrossing bands of burgundy accented with thinner bands of chartreuse and forest green. The "Heather Plaid" is a bit more desirable than the "Normandy" and is priced 15 to 20 percent higher. A "Normandy Plaid" 9¾-inch dinner plate should be valued at $22 to $26, and a cup and saucer at $18 to $22. Harder-to-find items include:

¼-pound butter dish, open	$80–$100
Oil and vinegar cruet	$75–$95
12-inch footed fruit bowl	$65–$85

"Intaglio"

This unusual pattern has narrow "S" shaped bands of lighter color undulating across a darker, solid color background. This is then accented with an etched image of a flower with leaves. On occasion, a different etched decoration such as a palm tree may occur. "Intaglio" is most often found in brown, but turquoise, baby blue, caramel, coral, and sapphire blue were made as well. Prices quoted here are for brown pieces; for turquoise examples add 20 percent, and for all others add 50 percent. Pieces with palm trees are more valuable also, and an example of this is the 16-ounce beer mug. In brown with an etched flower it is worth between $75 and $90, but with the palm tree, the value more than doubles to $165 to $225. A brown flower etched 9¾-inch dinner plate is $18 to $25, and a cup and saucer is $21 to $28. Hard-to-find items include:

8½-inch diameter luncheon plate with palm tree	$165–$225
Oval covered vegetable bowl	$120–$140
12¼-inch oblong divided platter	$85–$100

Roseville Pottery Company

This is an important name in the world of American pottery, but it is a company that is normally not associated with American everyday dinnerware. The Roseville Pottery Company was founded in Roseville, Ohio, in 1892. George Young, who previously had done everything from teaching school to selling Singer sewing machines without much success, became the new company's secretary and general manager. They bought out the old J. B. Owens factory and began making such things as flowerpots and stoneware storage jugs. Roseville was a success and in 1898 began expanding by buying other pottery companies in the area. In 1898, they bought their

first plant in Zanesville, Ohio, and in 1902, they bought another. By 1910, they had left the town of Roseville and had moved their entire operation to Zanesville

Roseville started making hand-painted art ware about 1900, and these continued to be produced until the 1920s, when they were abandoned in favor of making molded wares with very little handwork that collectors refer to as "commercial art wares." In the early 1950s, Roseville was in deep financial trouble and the company was slowly slipping into bankruptcy. To try and save themselves, they decided to give dinnerware a try, hoping that it might rescue the company from oblivion. Unfortunately, it did not, and Roseville went out of business in 1954.

"Raymor"

Designed by Ben Seibel, "Raymor" was introduced in 1952 and was produced for only a short time. It is a solid color ware that came in a variety of colors in both a matte and a glossy finish. The matte finish colors are autumn brown (which many collectors call "chocolate"), terra cotta, beach gray, and avocado green. There are actually two shades of avocado green—a light version that looks like its name suggests and a darker version that collectors call "frogskin." Glossy pieces of "Raymor" have a mottled look to the glaze that the matte pieces do not have. The glossy pieces were made in the same colors as the matte glazed items, but the mottled glaze on the glossy items makes some of the hues look different. Other colors include contemporary white, robin's egg blue, and chartreuse. Of the colors, autumn brown is the most available, while "frogskin" is the most sought after by collectors. A 10½-inch diameter dinner plate (#152) is valued in the $35 to $45 range, and a cup and saucer is worth about the same. Hard-to-find items include:

Large coffeepot (#176)	*$250–$325*
(add another $125 to $175 for the pottery stand)	
Divided vegetable bowl (#165)	*$200–$300*
Round casserole with lid	*$70–$85*

| *Gravy boat* | $100–$125 |
| *14-inch oval platter* | $100–$125 |

NOTE: Be aware that there is Italian pottery marked "Raymor." It was imported into this country during the second half of the 20th century, and "Raymor" is reportedly the name of the importer. These are decorative items and not dinnerware, so these pieces should not be too confusing.

Royal China Company

The Royal China Company moved from Omaha, Nebraska, to Sebring, Ohio, in 1933 and began operations in the old E. H. Sebring Pottery Company in 1934. They made a wide variety of semiporcelain dinnerware, as well as kitchenware and premium items to be given away at grocery stores and gas stations. As a general rule, it is Royal's later production pieces from the 1950s and 1960s that interest collectors the most. Royal was bought by the Jeannette Glass Company in 1969 and ceased operations in 1986.

"Buck's Country"

Found only in shades of brown and yellow, this pattern has a border of stylized tulips that is reminiscent of the folk art that is often associated with the Pennsylvania Dutch of Buck's other counties in Pennsylvania. The image found in the center of the flatware shows two houselike buildings (one may be a barn) with trees and a boy flying a kite. This pattern originated in the 1950s and is marked with the words "Buck's County" crudely lettered on a two-board sign with a bird perched on top. The value of a 10-inch diameter dinner plate is $12 to $15, and a cup and saucer is $15 to $20. Hard-to-find pieces include:

13 3/8-inch diameter round serving plate	$50–$65
Gravy boat and underplate	$45–$60
12-inch diameter chop plate	$35–$45

"Colonial Homestead"

This Royal China pattern was designed by Gordon Parker and was reportedly first made sometime between 1950 and 1952. It was advertised by Sears Roebuck all through the 1960s and came in both green and gray, with the gray examples being far rarer and more valuable than the

green. This pattern has a wood-grain border resembling boards with nails driven in where the boards meet each other, and in the center is the image of a room with a beamed ceiling with a large stone fireplace as the focal point. There is a hooked rag rug on the floor and a kettle crane in the fireplace, with a long rifle above the mantel. In green, a dinner plate is worth $8 to $12, but in gray, the same plate is $18 to $22. A 9-inch luncheon plate in green is $15 to $18, but in gray it is $18 to $20. A cup and saucer in gray is $22 to $25, but one in green is just $8 to $12. Hard-to-find items include:

Round covered vegetable, gray	$110–$125
Round covered vegetable, green	$65–$80
12-inch chop plate, gray	$65–$75
3-cup teapot, green	$110–$125

"Currier and Ives"

This pattern was initially made as a premium for Atlantic and Pacific Tea Company (A & P) grocery stores. Like "Colonial Homestead," it was designed by Gordon Parker, and indications are that it was first made circa 1949/50, and it continued to be made until as late as 1983. The pieces feature a wide variety of "Currier and Ives" or nostalgic American scenes printed in blue and white, pink and white, green and white, and very rarely, black and white. Some black and brown pie plates can also be found with the black examples being worth approximately $50 and the brown ones $60. A green pie plate is $70. Blue and white is the most popular color scheme with collectors. Scenes include a house and ice skaters, a couple in a horse-drawn sleigh, a train, a boy at a well, a lady driving a buggy, an old gristmill, and a rare Rocky Mountain view. Most of the ordinary parts of a dinner service are fairly inexpensive in this pattern, but some of the accessory items are becoming rather valuable. The lamp with globe, for example, is $325 to $400, and an original clock (made from a 10-inch dinner plate) is worth $225 to $300. A Royal "Currier and Ives" pattern dinner plate is valued at approximately $8 to $10, but a 9-inch luncheon plate is worth much more at $22 to $25, and a 7-inch salad plate is $15 to $18. A cup with an angled handle and saucer is about the same price as the dinner plate. A tall cup with a round handle is worth a bit more at $12 to $15. Hard-to-find pieces include:

Mark used by Royal China on their "Currier and Ives" dinnerware.

Tab-handled covered casserole	$275–$325
3-cup teapot	$175–$225
11½-inch chop plate with rare Rocky Mountain scene	$75–$100
Mug	$25–$30
Sugar bowl and lid—both styles	$25–$30
Gravy boat	$60–$75
¼-pound butter dish	$85–$100

NOTE: The Scio Pottery Company of Scio, Ohio, also made a "Currier and Ives" pattern dinnerware. Many of the pieces are distinguished by the use of a double oxen yoke on the lid or on the rim. Scio's "Currier and Ives" is not as widely collected as the Royal pieces.

"Memory Lane"

This 1950s Royal pattern is found in rose and white and has a decoration that is somewhat reminiscent of mid-19th-century English transfer ware. It has a rich acorn and oak leaf border, and in the center of the flatware is a saltbox-style house among trees with water and cows in front. A 10-inch dinner plate should be valued at $12 to $15, but a 7-inch salad plate is $20 to $25. A cup and saucer is $10 to $15. Hard-to-find items include:

10¼-inch diameter round covered vegetable	$80–$100
4-cup teapot	$135–$150
Three-tier serving tray	$55–$65
Two-tier serving tray	$50–$60

"Old Curiosity Shop"

This is another Gordon Parker design with a quaint "old-time" theme that originated in the 1950s. It has a wood-

Royal China Company's "Currier and Ives" pattern plate, $8 to $10. Item courtesy of Kingston Pike Antique Mall, Knoxville, Tennessee.

grain border decorated with curved strap hinges and the image of gabled buildings in the center. It was produced only in green, and a 10-inch dinner plate is $9 to $12, but the 9-inch luncheon plate is $26 to $30, and the 7-inch salad plate is just a bit less at $24 to $28. A cup and saucer is the same price as the 10-inch dinner plate. Hard-to-find items include:

1¹/₂-quart round covered casserole	$140–$160
Two-tier serving tray	$50–$65
¹/₄-pound butter dish	$55–$70

"Willow"

Royal began producing a standard "Willow" pattern in the 1930s, but the design was applied using a rubber stamp. It was available in three colors—standard blue, red, and gold—and came with at least three border variations. These pieces can be identified by the pattern name above "Royal China" in a box with a crown above. The second version was introduced in the 1940s and was transfer printed rather than rubber stamped. It was manufactured until the company closed in 1986 and came in shades of blue (by far the most common), pink, green, and brown. Be aware that some of these Royal China "Willow" items were unmarked. Prices quoted here are for transfer-printed blue "Willow." Rubber-stamped pieces are 20 percent less. Prices for colors other than blue are higher, and at the current moment, quotations for "Pink Willow" is almost double the values of the blue. A 9¾-inch transfer-printed dinner plate in blue is $10 to $14, and a cup and saucer is $8 to $12. In pink, the same plate is $16 to $20, and the cup and saucer is $18 to $22. Hard-to-find items include:

Round covered vegetable	$90–$110
Teapot	$120–$140

Salem China Company

Like so many companies that made American dinnerware, the dating for the Salem Chain Company is not entirely clear. It was founded in Salem, Ohio, in 1898 and production of pottery began in 1899. The company was founded by Pat and John McNichol, Dan Cronin, and William Smith of East Liverpool, Ohio, who supposedly were not optimistic about the potential for the further expansion of the pottery business in East Liverpool. Initially, the company was not very successful and was in serious financial trouble when it was purchased by the Sebring family in 1918 as a business for Frank Sebring Jr. after his return from World War I. At the time, the Sebrings were an important force in American ceramics; they had opened their first pottery in East Liverpool in 1887.

The Salem China Company went into business making white graniteware, but they branched out into making earthenware, kitchen items, and semiporcelain dinnerware. Most sources say that Salem is still in business as a distribution company and that they stopped manufacturing in either 1960 or 1967. Much of the Salem dinnerware introduced in the 1930s and 1940s was designed by the company's art director, Victor Schreckengost, who is considered to be one of the most important ceramics designers of the 20th century.

There was a dating system used at Salem China that will give the date of manufacture of a piece right down to the quarter of the year in which it was made. The system

TRICORNE
By
Salem
U. S. PATENT
D. 94245

Salem China Company mark used on their "Tricorne" dinnerware.

uses numbers, stars, and letters. The numbers are for the year, and the stars signify the quarter of the year. For example, "55✶✶" would signify that the piece was made in the second quarter of 1955. A notation of just "55" with no stars means that the item was made in the last quarter of the year 1955. The letters found with the marks identify the decorator and are of little interest to most collectors.

Salem China is noted for the quality of their decal designs, but the name given to the same decal decoration tended to change depending on which Salem shape it was placed. For instance, a decal named "Petitpoint Basket" on the "Victory" shape is called "Sampler" when it appears on another shape, and "Flower Basket" when it is placed on still another. Several of the Salem shapes that appeal to collectors are:

"Freeform"

This very modern shape originated in the 1940s and was created by Victor Schreckengost. The plates and other flatware are simple round coupe shapes, but the teapot looks something like a long-nosed cartoon animal with a comma-shaped finial on the lid, tripod feet, and a U-shaped open-ended handle that looks like a tail. The cup has tripod feet as well and received a design patent—supposedly the first that had been issued in 50 years. Three very distinctive designs appear on "Freeform" shapes. The first, and perhaps the most interesting, is called "Primitive" and is reminiscent of cave drawings showing stylized humans chasing deer. The deer with antlers are rather fully drawn, but the human shapes look like stick figures doing ballet. The second design is called "Hopscotch" and consists of lines that converge to make abstract star shapes. The last design is "Southwind" and depicts windswept branches in charcoal with leaves of turquoise, burnt orange, and green/gold. A 10-inch dinner plate in "Freeform" is worth between $15 and $20, while a cup and saucer should be valued at about the same. Hard-to-find pieces include:

Teapot	$60–$75
Coffee server	$50–$70
14-inch oval platter	$50–$70
Round vegetable	$60–$75

"Godey Print" or "Godey Ladies"

This decal decoration appears on several Salem shapes including "Briar Rose" and "Century." This image typically features two women in mid-19th-century attire, which is based on the fashion prints that appeared in *Godey's Lady's Book,* which was published between 1830 and 1898. The decal is particularly charming on "Brian Rose" shapes (first introduced in 1932) because the embossed floral border seems to add to the charm of the images of the ladies in long, frilly gowns. Collectors are familiar with this decal on service plates, and one of these should be valued at approximately $30 to $35. Interestingly, a smaller 10½-inch dinner plate is worth about the same, as is the cup and saucer. Hard-to-find items include:

9-inch round covered vegetable	$130–$145
22-by-18-inch large oval platter	$140–$165
5-cup coffee pot	$135–$150
Cake plate	$85–$100

"Tricorne"

This is a very distinctive shape because the flatware pieces are all triangular with outcurving sides and the hollowware items have very angular handles. This pattern originated in 1934, and the first pieces were decorated with a shockingly bright solid color glaze called "mandarin red." The outside of the hollowware pieces were solid mandarin red, and the flatware had wide red bands around the rim. Later, decorations on flatware consisted of concentric bands of color on the "verge," or the area where the rim and center well meet. Colors used were coral red, royal blue, and artiste, which was platinum. Some of the decals were "Sailing," which featured sailboats in shades of red and gray; "Polo," which depicted a horse and rider in black outlined in gray and coral red; and "Dutch Petitpoint," which shows the image of a boy and a girl. Of all the "Tricorne" items, the mandarin red pieces are found the most easily. A 9-inch plate is $15 to $20, while the same size party plate with a ring in the center to hold a tumbler is the same price. Standard cups and saucers are the same price, while after-dinner cups and saucers are more than twice that value. Hard-to-find items include:

Casserole	$50–$65
Coffeepot	$75–$100

"Victory"

Like "Freeform," this elegant grouping was designed by Victor Schreckengost; it was first made in 1938. This pattern is characterized by the thin ribs of the flatware pieces and the vertical ribs around the bottom of the hollowware items. The handles on "Victory" tend to have a very circular feeling. "Victory" pieces can be found in solid colors of green, lipstick red, maroon, periwinkle blue, and yellow. The glory of this shape, however, is the decal decorations, which include "Colonial Fireside," four different scenes each centered around a fireside interior in shades of brown, tan, and green; "Doily Petitpoint," a depiction of lacy needlework with an elaborate floral center; "Godey Prints," three different poses of ladies based on pictures found in Louis Antoine Godey's *Godey's Lady's Book;* "Jane Adams," a "U" shaped wreath of flowers and leaves; and "Minuet," a lady and a gentleman in 18th-century costume dance surrounded by a circular wreath of pink roses. All of these plus several more have approximately the same value, and a 10-inch diameter dinner plate is $20 to $25, and a cup and saucer is $25 to $30. Hard-to-find items include:

Mustache cup	$45–$60
Covered casserole	$100–$120
12-inch oval diameter platter with handles	$55–$75
Sugar bowl	$40–$50

Sebring Pottery Company

The Sebring family established its first pottery in East Liverpool, Ohio, in 1887. The patriarch of the family was George A. Sebring, and he had five sons—Oliver, George E., Ellsworth H., Frank A., and Joseph. The family established several potteries in East Liverpool and in East Palestine, but in 1899, they decided to buy some land in Mahoning County, Ohio, and establish their own town, to which they gave their family name. Much of the family pottery business was moved to this new town of Sebring, Ohio, and the second plant to be built there was named the Sebring Pottery Company. Other Sebring potteries include Limoges China Company (which used the "Limoges" and "American Limoges" mark discussed elsewhere and went into production in 1903) and the French-Saxon China Company (established 1911). These companies cause problems for collectors because they shared shapes and decals, and there is some thought that they also shared marks from time to time—guess it was all in the family. Sebring produced semi-porcelain dinnerware, toilet ware, and specialties, plus some kitchenware and art ware in the 1930s. In 1923, Sebring caused a revolution in dinnerware when it introduced its "Ivory Porcelain." Before this time, dinnerware was customarily on a white body, but Sebring's new ivory-colored body took the industry by storm, and many companies adopted this body color for its dinnerware. Some of the designs desired by collectors include:

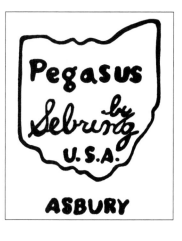

Mark used by the Sebring Pottery Company.

"Heirloom"

When this decal design is found on Sebring-marked items, it is called "Heirloom," but when it occurs on Limoges China Company items, it is called "Toledo Delight." This pattern features a lovely filigree around the border of the flatware items with a floral arrangement in the center surrounded by a lobed garland of flowers in the rococo manner. Often, it is found on Sebring's and Limoges' "Corinthian" or "Trojan" shapes, which have elegantly fluted edges on flatware and fluted sides on hollowware items. "Heirloom" and "Toledo Delight" can be found on both a white and an ivory background, with the white pieces being slightly more valuable than the ivory. For example, a 10-inch dinner plate in white is $24 to $30, but in ivory it is $20 to $25. The cup and saucer in white is $36 to $40, and in ivory, it is $30 to $35. Hard-to-find items include:

| Covered round vegetable, white | $140–$160 |
| Three-tier tidbit server, white | $65–$75 |

"Serenade"

This rococo-inspired decal features a garden setting with a man playing a lute while two women in 18th-century costume listen. It came on various Sebring shapes and with various border styles. One very distinctive style came with a bold burgundy border, but other examples can be found with a less colorful floral filigree border. Of the two border types mentioned, the burgundy is generally a bit more valuable than the floral filigree. The 10-inch dinner plate in the floral filigree is $18 to $22, while the same plate with the burgundy border is $20 to $25. Both styles of cups and saucers are $16 to $20. Hard-to-find items include:

| Three-tier tidbit tray, burgundy border | $55–$65 |
| 8 7/8-inch round vegetable bowl, floral filigree | $40–$50 |

Sterling China Company

Organized in Wellsville, Ohio, in 1917, the Sterling China Company was involved mainly in making dinnerware for institution purposes. They began by making vitreous hotel china in shapes such as bowls, mugs, and cups. During World War I, they produced a lot of dinnerware for the U.S. military. They are still in business today, and they might be something of a cipher in the minds of collectors if it had not been for the company's brief association with Russel Wright in 1949 (one source says 1948) and the designs that he produced for Sterling.

"Russel Wright"

There is some thought that Sterling tried to bridge the gap between dinnerware made for home use and dinnerware made for restaurants with this very appealing line. Wright's main involvement was to design the shapes and select the colors. He did a brilliant job of creating shapes that would be advantageous for restaurateurs in that the plates had a rolled rim that made them easy to grasp and not slip out of servers' hands, and the lids had recessed finger grips that allowed them to be easily—and securely—handled. In addition, these pieces were sturdy and practical and often were designed to be used for more than one purpose. The colors that Wright chose for his designs were ones that he thought would look good with food—ivy green, straw yellow, suede gray, and cedar brown. Sterling also produced Wright's designs in standard white for the restaurant trade and shell pink— but that was a corporate rather than a design decision. Wright's association with Sterling ended after approximately one year, but the company continued to manu-

Sterling China Company's Wright Mark.

facture items using his designs long after the great industrial designer had departed. Wright designed some decorations for this ware, notably a line called "Polynesian," with palm trees and other Hawaiian and Asian themes that were meant for the Shun Lee Dynasty Restaurant in New York City. Sterling's art department, however, supplied most of the designs to fit their institutional customers' needs. For example, the Carnation Milk Company's restaurants had carnations placed on the pieces they ordered, and other companies chose to have their name emblazoned on the items they purchased for their establishments. Some of these designs can be very appealing, and they provide a great deal of variety for collectors to find. Enthusiasts who are interested in collecting Sterling's "Russel Wright" dinnerware need to be aware that not all pieces are marked, and large quantities do not bear the Sterling "Russel Wright" mark shown on page 144 but have a more generic Sterling backstamp instead. The rarest color in this line is shell pink and it is 50 percent more valuable than the other colors. The next most desired color is ivy green, and prices for this hue are at the top end of the scale. A 10¼-inch dinner plate in colors other than shell pink is $15 to $20, and a regular 7-ounce cup and saucer is $18 to $26. Hard-to-find items include:

3½-ounce after-dinner cup and saucer	$65–$85
Coffee bottle	$125–$150
10-ounce teapot	$125–$150

Stetson China Company

Louis Stetson was an ambitious Polish immigrant who initially worked in his uncle's clothing store in Chicago, Illinois. Stetson learned that money could be made buying undecorated china "blanks" or "whiteware" adding decal or hand-painted decoration and reselling it. He made an arrangement with the Mt. Clemens Pottery Company of Mt. Clemens, Michigan, to purchase "blanks." This venture was successful, and Louis Stetson brought in his nephew Joe from Poland, who eventually took over the company after Louis' death. Stetson also bought "blanks" from the Illinois China Company in Lincoln, Illinois, and in 1946 they purchased this company to assure themselves a steady supply of china. It should be mentioned that Stetson bought odd lots of decals to use on its dinnerware, and these decorations can make Stetson products look very much like the wares from other companies. For a time, however, Stetson discontinued the use of decals and started doing hand painting under glaze in the style of Southern Potteries ("Blue Ridge") and Red Wing. Stetson went so far as to hire away decorators from these two firms, and such patterns as "Cynthia" (circa 1949) are very similar to "Blue Ridge" designs. Many later wares made at Stetson were sold to jobbers who in turn sold them to furniture stores, gas stations, and grocery stores to be used as premiums. Stetson closed in 1965 (one source says 1966).

"Golden Empress"

This pattern was a favorite for store premiums and is distinguished by its wide gold border with filigree accents. Various decals were used to decorate these pieces, but one of the most commonly found has the image of a lady and a gentleman in 18th-century dress (the gentleman is holding a tricorn hat) dancing with a musician in the background. It should be noted that this decoration appears on the wares of several other dinnerware makers. A 10-inch dinner plate in this pattern is valued in the $28 to $32 range, and a cup and saucer is $22 to $26. Hard-to-find items include:

13 3/8 inch oval platter $65–$75

"Lady Marlow" and "Duchess of Greencastle"

These decal decoration are very similar. "Lady Marlow" has a wide burgundy border with a red rose in the center, and on flatware pieces, a black "V" shaped accent between the colored border and the white well that looks like stitching. "Duchess of Greencastle." on the other hand, has a wide green border surrounding a floral center which has been described as a "laurel" blossom, but the leaves make it look like a white rose. It also has the black "V" shaped accents between border and well. In general, "Lady Marlow" is a bit more expensive

One of Stetson China Company's marks.

than "Duchess of Greencastle," with a "Lady Marlow" cup and saucer and 10-inch dinner plate being valued at $26 to $30. A "Duchess of Greencastle" cup and saucer and 10-inch dinner plate is $18 to $22. Hard-to-find items include:

13½-inch oval platter, "Lady Marlowe"	$70–$85
Round covered vegetable, "Duchess of Greencastle"	$110–$125
8¾-inch round vegetable, "Lady Marlowe"	$50–$65
8¾-inch round vegetable, "Duchess of Greencastle"	$42–$50

Steubenville Pottery Company

Organized in Steubenville, Ohio, in 1879, this company was immediately successful and had seven firing and six glost kilns going by 1889. By the early 20th century, they were making graniteware, semiporcelain, and true porcelain and turning out both dinnerware and and sanitary ware. Financial trouble struck Steubenville in the 1950s, and pieces marked "Final Kiln" were produced in December 1959.

This, however, is where the story becomes confusing because Steubenville's molds, equipment, and name were sold to the Barium Chemical Company, which then sold them to the Canonsburg Pottery Company of Canonsburg, Pennsylvania. This company had been started by W. S. George in 1900 as the Canonsburg China Company. In 1909, it changed hands and became the Canonsburg Pottery with John George, W. S. George's brother, as president.

Canonsburg produced dinnerware from the Steubenville molds after 1959, and pieces can be found marked with a script "Steubenville" signature similar to the one used by the original company. Occasionally, marks will read "The Steubenville Division Canonsburg Pottery Co.," but the script signature marks without this notation can be very confusing. Canonsburg closed in 1979, and current collectors are interested in these pre-1959 Steubenville lines:

"Adam Antique"

Designed in the style associated with English architect and designer James Adam (1728–1792), this dinnerware is distinguished by an embossed border consisting of covered neoclassical urns interlaced with garlands and leaves. In addition, the rims of the flatware pieces are gadrooned. This pattern was introduced in 1932, and the creamy white examples with no other decoration look very much like an English pattern that would have been made by a company such as Wedgwood. Steubenville, however, did decorate "Adam Antique" with a number of different floral decals. A 10-inch dinner plate in this pattern is worth $20 to $15, and a cup and saucer is $14 to $18. Hard-to-find pieces include:

Round covered vegetable	$70–$85
Coffeepot	$85–$100
Chop plate	$40–$50
15-inch oval serving platter	$55–$70

"American Modern"

It is reported that Steubenville made more than 125 million pieces of this line, which was designed by Russel Wright (another source, however, says the number is closer to 70 million). "American Modern," which originated in late 1939 and was made until Steubenville closed in 1959, is said to be the first mass-produced dinnerware created by an industrial designer. It was a hit from the start, and in 1941 it was named the best ceramic design of the year by the American Designers' In-

stitute. Initially it came in six colors—seafoam blue, granite gray, chartreuse curry, coral, bean brown, and white. During World War II, bean brown was dropped. Black chutney came into the lineup around 1950 or 1951, and about this same time, seafoam blue was dropped and cedar green added. Other colors include Steubenville blue, cantaloupe, and glacier blue, which is a powder blue flecked with a darker blue. The most sought-after colors are bean brown, cantaloupe, glacier blue, white, and Steubenville blue (Steubenville blue is an undocumented color that turns up from time to time). The least desired colors are granite gray and coral, and pieces in these shades can be much less valuable than similar pieces in the top five colors. It is important to note that "American Modern" dinnerware is subject to crazing, and pieces that have suffered this glaze degradation are greatly devalued. Decorated examples of "American Modern" were made but generally do not command a premium price. A 10-inch dinner plate in coral is valued in the $10 to $15 range, and one in granite gray is a few dollars more. A dinner plate in glacier blue is $50 to $60, and one in bean brown is $25 to $35. A regular cup and saucer is $10 to $12 in coral and a few dollars more in granite gray. In glacier blue, a regular cup and saucer is $25 to $35, and in bean brown $22 to $32.

Hard-to-find items include:

Carafe in bean brown	*$350–$450*
Carafe in bean brown with original wooden stopper	*$800–$1,200*
Covered casserole in Steubenville blue	*$1,200–$1,400*
Tall water pitcher, cantaloupe	*$550–$650*
13-inch square chop plate, glacier blue	*$100–$120*
13-inch oval divided vegetable bowl, cedar green	*$140–$160*
4-cup teapot, granite gray	*$160–$175*
2-cup coffeepot, white	*$225–$250*
Stack set, two bowls and a lid, granite gray	*$400–$450*

"Betty Pepper"

This is a plain shape that was introduced in 1939 and was made for the member department stores of the Associated Merchandising Corporation. These stores included the prestigious Bloomingdale's in New York City, Hudson's in Detroit, Michigan, and Joseph Horne in Philadelphia, Pennsylvania. "Betty Pepper" came decorated with a variety of mostly floral decals and is marked with a "Betty Pepper" signature and the word "dinnerware" above a house and an "A. M. C." monogram. No mention is made of its manufacturer, Steubenville. This is a very "short" line of dinnerware, with only a dozen or so items. A 9-inch dinner plate is $15 to $20, and a cup and saucer is a bit less at $12 to $15. Hard-to-find items include:

2-cup teapot	$40–$60
Gravy boat with underplate	$30–$40
Casserole	$50–$75

"Shalimar"

This solid color dinnerware is subtly decorated with a light embossed pattern of flowers, tendrils, and leaves that shows an Islamic influence. It was first produced in 1938 and was made in beige/ivory, pink, and blue/gray. One source reports that there was also a white, but this may have reference to the soft blue/gray. Pieces are marked "Shalimar by Steubenville." This pattern is a little difficult to find, and a 9-inch dinner plate is valued at $36 to $40, and a cup and saucer at $30 to $38. Hard-to-find items include:

Coffeepot	$120–$140
12-inch chop plate	$48–$60

"Woodfield"

This is another Steubenville solid color pattern, but this one is distinguished by the leaf pattern found on hollowware pieces and the leaf-shaped plates. This pattern was made using many of the same glazes found on "American Modern." When this design first appeared in 1941, the colors were dove gray, golden fawn, jungle green, and salmon pink. Although it is not apparent from the name, golden fawn is chartreuse. In 1951, rust and tropic green were added. Rust is probably the rarest color in this line, and jungle green and tropic green are desired shades also. This line is known for its snack or party plate sets. These came in two sizes, and Steubenville called the smallest of these cup and plate pairs a "Tea and Toast," while the larger ones were dubbed a "Video Set." A 10-inch dinner plate in "Woodfield" is valued in the range of $12 to $18, while a cup and saucer is a bit more at $14 to $20. A "Tea and Toast" party plate is $10 to $14, and a "Video Set" plate is $16 to $20. Hard-to-find pieces include:

Two-part relish dish	$40–$50
Fork and spoon (serving)	$125–$150
13½-inch chop plate	$60–$80
6-cup teapot	$80–$100

Univeral Potteries, Incorporated

The history of this company begins with the Bradshaw China Company, which was organized in Niles, Ohio, in 1901 and made semiporcelain dinnerware, toilet sets, and novelties. It was sold to the Sebring family sometime between 1912 and 1916 and then sold again in 1921. For a brief period, it was called Crescent China Company, but that was quickly changed to the Atlas China Company. This firm then merged with the Globe Pottery of Cambridge, Ohio, to become the Atlas Globe China Company.

The owner of Atlas Globe also owned the Oxford Pottery in Cambridge, which manufactured brown kitchenwares such as bean pots, custard cups, and teapots made from the red clay mined on land surrounding the factory. In 1934, there was a reorganization that consolidated two companies with Oxford Pottery, absorbing the financially troubled Atlas Globe China Company and changing the company name to Universal Potteries, Incorporated. Universal made dinnerware until 1956, when it shifted its emphasis to making floor and wall tiles and became the Oxford Tile Company Division of Universal Potteries. Final closure came in 1960. Some of the Universal items most desired by collectors are:

"Ballerina"

The most important shape made by Universal was named "Ballerina," which can be identified easily by the mark that features the name and the image of a dancer in toe shoes and a tutu. This line originated in the late 1940s, and the original solid colors were jade green, jonquil yellow, periwinkle blue, and dove gray. Chartreuse and forest green were added in 1949, and in 1955, pink, burgundy, and charcoal made their appearance. Sierra rust is the final solid color used on "Ballerina" shapes, but there is no information as to exactly when it was added to the line. A wide variety of decals were used on "Ballerina," and they are usually found on an ivory background. A "Ballerina" 10-inch diameter dinner plate is valued at $15 to $20, and a cup and saucer is $16 to $22. Hard-to-find pieces include:

Round covered vegetable	$90–$110
Gravy boat	$40–$65
Handled cake plate	$45–$60
13-inch diameter chop plate	$60–$70

"Calico Fruit"

This charming decal decoration has attracted a lot of collector interest. The center design consists of a straight-sided blue bowl that contains a pile of fruit shapes that appear to be made from colorful fabric. The fruit appears to spill out on the surface surrounding the bowl, and most of the pieces with this design are accented with a red line that runs around rims and edges. This pattern was sold in department stores, such as Montgomery Ward, and there is matching metalware and glassware available. Unfortunately, this decal often tends to fade rather badly, and it is sometimes hard to find examples with the decals in good condition. The flatware in this pattern is rather expensive, and a dinner plate is valued in the $60 to $70 range, while a 9½-inch diameter plate is $40 to $50, and a 7¼-inch plate is $35 to $40. A cup and saucer is $50 to $60. Hard-to-find items include:

Mark used by Universal Potteries, Incorporated, on its "Ballerina" dinnerware.

14-inch oval platter	$90–$110
Pie server	$60–$75
Large refrigerator jar	$80–$100

"Cattail"

NOTE: The dictionary prefers "Cattail," but the advertising of the day tended to print the name as "Cat-Tail" or even "Cat Tail." We choose to go with the dictionary and use "Cattail."

This is one of the most popular decal patterns found on Universal's "Ballerina" shapes, but this design can be found also on other Universal shapes, such as "Cam-

wood" and "Mt. Vernon." The "Cattail" pattern was very simple and consisted of the image of a grouping of red cattails with green leaves and stems. There was usually a red line border around the edge of these pieces, but occasionally a red and black line will occur. The "Cattail" decal was apparently introduced in the 1930s and continued to be used for some time into the 1940s and beyond. It was used by Universal on a variety of shapes, including "Camwood," "Old Holland," "Laurella," "Mt. Vernon," and of course, "Ballerina." Just as the "Autumn Leaf" decal was not an exclusive of the Hall China Company, "Cattail" was not an exclusive of Universal Potteries. Other manufacturers used the design as well, and in the 1940s, Sears, Roebuck offered a kitchen table, four chairs, and a nine-piece luncheon tablecloth and napkins set all decorated with the "Cattail" pattern plus a 32-piece set of "Cattail" dinnerware for $23.89. Also available were everything from a garbage can to a kitchen scale—all smartly emblazoned with the "Cattail" design. A 10-inch dinner plate should be valued in the $20 to $40 range, depending on the Universal shape on which the "Cattail" decal appears, and a cup and saucer is worth $20 to $35. Hard-to-find items include:

1-pound butter dish	*$50–$65*
Syrup jug with a chrome top	*$60–$75*
Round covered vegetable dish	*$100–$125*
Pie serving plate	*$60–$75*
32-ounce pitcher	*$50–$65*

"Laurella"

Introduced in 1948, this solid color line had laurel leaves embossed around the edge. It came in four pastel colors—cocotan (i.e., cocoa/tan), jade (green), jonquil (yellow), and periwinkle (blue). A 10-inch dinner plate should be valued in the $16 to $20 range, and a cup and saucer is the same. Pieces should be marked with a circular Universal mark with the name "Laurella" at the top and the words "Oven Proof." Hard-to-find pieces include:

9-inch round vegetable bowl	*$32–$38*
13³/₄-inch round chop plate	*$30–$35*
Gravy boat and underliner	*$55–$65*

"Woodvine"

This was an attractive line that featured small red/orange star-shaped flowers among larger two-toned green leaves. This was used by Universal as a "booster line," meaning that grocery stores used it as a premium to boost their sales. "Woodvine" is reportedly Universal's most popular "booster line" of the 1930s and 1940s. A 10-inch dinner plate is $14 to $18, and a cup and saucer is $15 to $20. Hard-to-find pieces include:

9-inch salad serving bowl	*$60–$70*
9-inch oval vegetable bowl	*$40–$50*
9-inch round vegetable bowl	*$50–$60*
Gravy boat	*$65–$75*

4

THE INSTANT EXPERT'S GUIDE TO CONTINUING EDUCATION

For collectors, the old cliché "knowledge is power" could not be truer. The more you know, the more treasures you will be able to find at auctions, estate sales, flea markets, and antique shops.

The more you know, the less likely you are to buy a reproduction or to spend too much money on an item that is not as rare as it might seem to be. And the more you know, the less likely you are to pass up an item that is extremely rare because it does not "ring a bell." In short, those who do not do their homework may find themselves at a great disadvantage in the marketplace.

Seasoned collectors always say that books make them money, and they can certainly make collecting more fun. What follows is a list of books that should be helpful to anyone interested in learning more about American everyday dinnerware.

Recommended Reading and Bibliography

Chipman, Jack. *The Collector's Encyclopedia of Bauer Pottery Identification and Values*. Paducah, Ky.: Collector Books, 1998.

Cunningham, Jo. *The Collector's Encyclopedia of American Dinnerware*. Paducah, Ky.: Collector Books, 1982.

Dollen, B. L., and R. L. Dollen. *Red Wing Art Pottery Book II*. Paducah, Ky.: Collector Books, 1998.

Duke, Harvey. *Official Price Guide to Pottery and Porcelain*, 8th ed. New York: House of Collectibles/Random House Reference, 1995.

Elliot-Bishop, James F. *Franciscan, Catalina, and Other Gladding, McBean Wares: Ceramic Table and Art Wares, 1873–1942*. Atglen, Pa.: Schiffer Publishing Ltd., 2001.

Gibbs, Carl Jr. *The Collector's Encyclopedia of Metlox Potteries*. Paducah, Ky.: Collector Books, 2001.

The Homer Laughlin Collectors Association. *Fiesta, Harlequin, Kitchen Kraft: The Homer Laughlin Collectors Association Guide*. Atglen, Pa.: Schiffer Publishing Ltd., 2000.

Huxford, Bob, and Sharon Huxford. *The Collector's Encyclopedia of Fiesta*. Paducah, Ky.: Collector Books, 1992.

Huxford, Bob, and Sharon Huxford. *The Collector's Encyclopedia of Fiesta Plus Harlequin, Riviera and Kitchen Kraft*. Paducah, Ky.: Collector Books, 2001.

Huxford, Bob, and Sharon Huxford. *The Collector's Encyclopedia of Roseville Pottery*. Paducah, Ky.: Collector Books, 1972.

Keller, Joe, and David Ross. *Russel Wright Dinnerware, Pottery and More: An Identification and Price Guide*. Atglen, Pa.: Schiffer Publishing Ltd., 2000.

Lehner, Louise. *Lehner's Encyclopedia of U.S. Marks on Pottery, Porcelain and Clay*. Paducah, Ky.: Collector Books, 1988.

Miller, C. L. *The Jewel Tea Company: Its History and Products*. Atglen, Pa.: Schiffer Publishing Ltd., 1994.

Nelson, Maxine. *Versatile Vernon Kilns: An Illustrated Value Guide Book II*. Paducah, Ky.: Collector Books, 1983.

Newbound, Betty, and Bill Newbound. *Best of Blue Ridge Dinnerware Identification and Value Guide*. Paducah, Ky.: Collector Books, 2003.

Pratt, Michael. *Mid-Century Modern Dinnerware: A Pictorial Guide*. Atglen, Pa.: Schiffer Publishing Company Ltd., 2003.

Racheter, Richard. *Post 86 Fiesta Identification and Value Guide*. Paducah, Ky.: Collector Books, 2001.

Reiss, Ray. *Red Wing Dinnerware Price and Identification Guide*. Chicago: Property Publishing, 1997.

Rinker, Harry L. *Dinnerware of the 20th Century: The Top 500 Patterns*. New York: House of Collectibles/Crown Publishing Group, 1997.

Snyder, Jeffrey B. *Depression Pottery*. Atglen, Pa.: Schiffer Publishing Ltd., 1999.

Stern, Bill. *California Pottery from Mission to Modernism*. San Francisco: Chronicle Books, 2001.

Collectors' Clubs, Newsletters, and Web Sites

What follows is a list of places where collectors can find more information about American everyday dinnerware. Many of these will be Web sites because in today's world that is the way a great deal of the available knowledge about a given subject is disseminated.

Be advised, however, that the information available on the Internet is not always the best, and facts obtained in this manner should be checked with other—usually printed—sources.

Also, please keep in mind that these sites and addresses go out-of-date very quickly. This is the most current information that could be found, but after even one year from the date of publication of this book some of it will have changed.

www.bauerpottery.com
This site contains information about publications, articles, the Bauer line, and the marketplace. It may be somewhat out-of-date since the last update was in late 2002.

Bauer Quarterly
This magazine is no longer being printed, but back copies are available by writing Paul Preston, *Bauer Quarterly*, P.O. Box 2524, Berkeley, CA 95702-0524.

Blue Ridge Collectors Club
208 Harris Street, Erwin, TN 37650.

www.colling.com
A Vernon Kilns site that offers information about the company, identification of patterns, chat with other collectors, and the opportunity to post want lists. This site also covers Garden City Pottery and Winfield Pottery.

www.dedhampottery.com
This Web site offers information on Dedham Pottery and Dedham reproductions plus a newsletter. The newsletter may be obtained by writing Dedham Pottery Collectors Society, c/o Jim Kaufman, 248 Highland Street, Dedham, MA 02065-5833.

www.earthstationnine.com
Under "pottery," this huge site has information about such firms and patterns as Bauer, Blue Ridge, Dedham, Eva Zeisel, "Fiesta," "Franciscan Ware," Hall China, Harker, Homer Laughlin, Metlox, Red Wing, Roseville, Stangl, and Vernon Kilns.

Fiesta Club of America
P.O. Box 15383, Machesney Park, IL 61115-5383. This club offers a newsletter.

Fiesta Collectors Club
P.O. Box 471, Valley City, OH 44280.

www.gmcb.com
This site will take you to the *Franciscan Newsletter* with information on Gladding, McBean's "Franciscan" dinnerware.

www.goldenstateredwing.com
This is the California branch of the Red Wing Collectors Society. They call themselves the "Golden State Wing Nuts" and produce a beautiful newsletter.

Hall China Collectors Newsletter
P.O. Box 360488, Cleveland, OH 44136.

www.hlcca.org
This is the Web site of the Homer Laughlin China Collectors Association. There is a quarterly magazine entitled *The Dish*. Written correspondence can be directed to HLCCA, P.O. Box 1093, Corbin, KY 40702-1093.

www.inter-services.com/hallchina
This site is all about collecting Hall China, with a bulletin board and a trader section.

The LuRay Relay
204 South Veitch #3, Arlington, VA 22204. A newsletter devoted to "Lu-Ray" dinnerware.

www.nalcc.org
This is the Web site for the National Autumn Leaf Collectors Club. They can be reached by mail at NALCC, P.O. Box 7929, Moreno Valley, CA 92552-7929. They publish a newsletter.

www.ohioriverpottery.com
This is an American dinnerware identification site that boasts more than 600 pages and 2,700 illustrations.

www.redwingcollectors.org
This is the national Red Wing Collectors Society, and they produce a newsletter.

www.replacements.com
This is the Web site for Replacements, Ltd., located in Greensboro, North Carolina. They are primarily a replacements service, but they list hundreds of companies and probably thousands of dinnerware patterns, and a perusal can help establish retail values for a collection of dinnerware and can also provide a source for missing pieces.

Roseville of the Past Pottery Club
P.O. Box 656, Clariona, FL 32710-0656.

groups.yahoo.com/group/russelwright
This site connects to the Russel Wright Discussion Group.

www.stanglfulper.com
This is the Web site for the Stangl Fulper Collectors Club.

www.the1950s.com/rworphan
This Web site offers information on Russel Wright designs and a list of items that people want to sell.

www.willowcollectors.org
This collectors' club for "Blue Willow" pattern dinnerware can be reached at 503 Chestnut Street, Perkasie, PA 18944.

5

THE INSTANT EXPERT'S QUIZ

1. A set of two rectangular pitchers on a tray—one to hold hot water, the other tea—is known as a what?

2. Name two other companies besides the Hall China Company that used the famous "Autumn Leaf" decal.

3. What famous English company founded in the 18th century now owns the former Gladding, McBean & Company?

4. The design for Gladding, McBean's "Apple" dinnerware was taken from what line made by which important maker of American art pottery?

5. In what year was Hall's "Autumn Leaf" first made?

6. Name the other pattern Hall made for Jewel Tea.

7. Industrial designer Russel Wright designed a number of dinnerware lines for several different companies. What was the name of the Russel Wright line manufactured by Harker?

8. In the Homer Laughlin dating system, what would the designation "F 28 R" on a piece of dinnerware indicate?

9. Why did Homer Laughlin discontinue making their red "Fiesta" color?

10. The name "Metlox" was obtained from what two words?

11. What are the names of the two rarest shapes used by Southern Potteries to make "Blue Ridge" dinnerware?

12. Who is credited with making the first solid color dinnerware in America other than plain white?

13. What is the name of the dinnerware that is thought to be Taylor, Smith and Taylor's attempt to compete with Homer Laughlin's "Fiesta"?

14. Name two men who were responsible for dinnerware designs made at Vernon Kilns.

15. Name two Hollywood movies that inspired Vernon Kilns dinnerware patterns.

16. Name two lines that greatly influenced Homer Laughlin's "Fiesta."

17. In Dedham's "Crackleware," what is the most commonly found pattern?

18. What is the other name given to W. S. George's "Breakfast Nook" pattern?

19. Ben Seibel designed five dinnerware lines for Iroquois. Which one is the rarest?

20. What company is credited with using the first underglaze decal decoration?

21. What is the name of the dinnerware line that the famous Roseville Pottery Company hoped would save them from bankruptcy?

22. When and where did the Sebring family establish their first pottery-making operation?

23. The first mass-produced dinnerware created by an industrial designer was made by what company and is known by what name?

24. Name three of the "go-along" items that were made with the "Cattail" design found on Universal Potteries dinnerware.

25. What dinnerware line was created in 1940 for an exhibition at New York City's Metropolitan Museum of Art?

Answers to the Instant Expert's Quiz

1. Cozy set.

2. Crown Pottery, W. S. George, Columbia Chinaware, Vernon Kilns, and Paden City.

3. Wedgwood.

4. "Zona" by Weller.

5. 1933.

6. "Cameo Rose."

7. "White Clover."

8. That the piece was made in June 1928 in either Laughlin's #6 or #7 plant.

9. Because they could not obtain the uranium oxide needed to make it—not because it was mildly radioactive.

10. "Metallic" and "oxide."

11. "Trellis" and "Waffle."

12. Fulper.

13. "Vistosa."

14. Rockwell Kent, Walt Disney, Don Blanding, Gale Turnbill, Paul Davidson.

15. *Fantasia* and *Winchester '73*.

16. Bauer's "Ring" and Gladding, McBean's "El Patio."

17. Right-facing "Rabbit."

18. "Springtime."

19. "Interplay."

20. Paden City Pottery Company.

21. "Raymor."

22. 1887, East Liverpool, Ohio.

23. Steubenville Pottery Company, "American Modern."

24. Luncheon tablecloth, napkins, table, chairs, garbage can, and kitchen scales.

25. "Metropolitan" by Gladding, McBean.

INDEX

A

Aaron family, 50
"Adam Antique," 146, 147
Akron China Co., 3
Allen, Bob, 65, 67
"Amber Glo," 89
American China Co., 3
"American Modern," 146, 146–48, 148
"American Traditional," 69
"Americana," 51–52
"Anniversary," 82
"Antique Grape," 65, 73
"Apple," 27–29, 28, 31, 68, 130
"Ardennes," 80
"Argosy," 118
"Astor," 84
Atlas Globe China Co., 150
"Autumn Apple," 86
"Autumn Bloom," 69
"Autumn Leaf," vii, 18, 20–23, 37–39, 38, 40
"Aztec," 66, 122

B

backstamp, 4–5, 5
baker, 5, 6
"Ballerina," 150–52, 151–52
"Basketweave," 116–17
batter set, 5
Bauer, George, 44
Bauer, John Andrew, 108–9
Beale, Joseph Boggs, 59
Bennett, James, 43
Bennison, Faye, 98
"Betty Pepper," 148–49
bisque, 5
Blanding, Don, 98, 103, 104
blank, 5
"Blue Bouquet," 40
"Blue Diamonds," 123
"Blue Doves," 122
"Blue Ridge," 83–88, 84, 144
"Blue Vineyard," 122

"Blueberry," 89
"Bob White," 78, 78
"Bolero," 116, 117
bouillon cup, 5, 7, 9
"Bouquet," 42
Bradshaw China Co., 150
"Breakfast Nook," 116, 117–18
"Briar Rose," 139
British royal coat of arms, 3, 3
"Brittany," 79–80, 86
"Brown-Eyed Susan," 47, 98–99, 99
"Bucks County," 133

C

"Calico Fruit," 151
"Caliente," 124–25, 126
California, 2, 26, 64
"California Apple" and "Fruit," 67
"California Colored Pottery," 109, 111
"California Contempora,"
"Freeform," and "Mobile," 66
"California Golden Blossom," 67
"California Ivy," 65, 67
"California Peach Blossom," 67–68, 68, 74
"California Pottery," 65
"California Provincial," 71–72
"Camellia," 68–69
"Cameo Rose," 40
"Cameoware," 44, 44–46, 49
"Camwood," 151–52
"Candlewick," 84
Canonsburg Pottery Co., 145–46
"Capistrano," 82
"Carrara Modern," 120
"Carv-kraft," 45
casserole, 5, 7, 11
casting, 6
"Castle," 94
"Casual," 78, 79, 81
"Casual China," 120–22, 121–22
Catalina Pottery, 35